GRITS

ALSO BY ERIN BYERS MURRAY

Shucked:
Life on a New England Oyster Farm

GRITS

A Cultural and Culinary Journey
Through the South

✳

ERIN BYERS MURRAY

St. Martin's Press
New York

GRITS. Copyright © 2018 by Erin Byers Murray. All rights reserved.
Printed in the United States of America. For information, address
St. Martin's Press, 175 Fifth Avenue, New York, N.Y. 10010.

www.stmartins.com

Design by Kathryn Parise

The Library of Congress Cataloging-in-Publication Data is available upon request.

ISBN 978-1-250-11607-9 (hardcover)
ISBN 978-1-250-11608-6 (ebook)

Our books may be purchased in bulk for promotional, educational, or business use.
Please contact your local bookseller or the Macmillan Corporate and Premium
Sales Department at 1-800-221-7945, extension 5442, or by email at
MacmillanSpecialMarkets@macmillan.com.

First Edition: November 2018

10   9   8   7   6   5   4   3   2   1

This book is dedicated to Charlie & Maggie.
May your lives be rich with love, stories, and good food.

CONTENTS

PROLOGUE

My story doesn't start with grits. Although I was born in Augusta, Georgia, I grew up for the most part living outside the South—more than thirty years in places where grits were not a thing. I ate grits now and then as a kid but, unlike scores of folks in the South and beyond, I can't claim to have been raised on grits.

I've since come to appreciate them, just as I've come to better understand and appreciate the South. When I set out to write this book, I put myself on an intentional quest to do both. Along the way, I met corn farmers, seed savers, food writers, millers, grit packers, home cooks, historians, and Southern chefs who all helped me understand that, like many foods, grits help tell a story of the South. It's a story that is not just about a pile of food on a plate. It goes deeper. It's at once joyful, sustaining, delicious, divisive, painful, and funny.

Grits reflect certain traits that I love about the South—they can be a simple celebration of humble, home-kitchen cooking or they can be dressed up, rethought, and revamped, interpreted into a more modern rendition. But grits also reveal storylines of the South's most conflicted realities—they are intertwined with the region's history of genocide and slavery and the resulting racial, cultural, class, and gender disparities that still exist.

I returned to the South to make Nashville my home in 2012, after longing for it for almost a decade. That is not an uncommon thing. Many people I've met and read about since moving from Boston to Nashville share my story: We left the South—whether pushed or pulled for reasons out of our control, like me, or driven by the urge to break free, or by the calling of opportunity or the desire to travel—and then found ourselves wanting to get back, to reconnect, to better understand this evolving region.

In many cases, I found that things had changed. Communities were larger, more colorful, more diverse—and yet many still retained their Southern lilt, as though the newest arrivals, who hailed from countries near and far, had adopted, and were feeding off, the history, the culture, the soul they found rising up out of the heat and earth of their new Southern grounds.

Upon my return, I also found a region that was both welcoming and guarded, accepting of strangers but with a quiet wariness that floated between statements like "What brought you back?" and "How are you liking it?" It was as if Southerners were waiting to see whether I would adapt and fit in—or whether I was better suited back where I'd been. Part of me assumed that my assimilation back to the South would come easily, like picking up an old recipe card and knowing inherently when to add a little extra sugar. Instead, it was like tackling Escoffier without the translation.

My context, which had been shaped in youth and reframed over and over again by my own nostalgia for the place—and especially its foods—was out of whack. Before moving back and setting out on this project, I hadn't considered the many weights, measures, and historical realities that sit upon the Southern dishes I hold dear.

Grits can channel emotions and memories, and evoke tradition, no matter whether they're found on restaurant menus, breakfast tables, at church picnics, cocktail parties, or community potlucks. And I've learned that those who cook, eat, produce, write, and talk about grits are helping to shape an evolving story about the South.

The South is vast and diverse. It's made up of myriad micro regions, all of which are calling to be understood and celebrated in their own way. Nashville is now known for more than its neon call of honkytonks or the flaming crunch of hot chicken—today, it supports a dining scene that includes a growing number of Kurdish markets and Korean street food trucks alongside its meat and threes. It's hard to compare that evolution in any way to what's happening on the coast of South Carolina, where oyster beds are still tonged at sunrise and the foods of the Gullah Geechee are being acknowledged and celebrated. There's long been a multicultural food scene supported by the stony streets of New Orleans, and in North Carolina's Piedmont region, an area known for its barbecue and boiled peanuts, the culture can now be better understood through its new abundance of farm-focused, chef-driven restaurants. Each of these micro regions is becoming better defined as we explore Southern food—and grits have played a role in many of those story lines.

When I first set out on this project I assumed there was a divide between those who ate grits and those who didn't—and that the divide ran about even with the same line drawn by Mason and Dixon. But as I researched and interviewed, ate, and wrote, I came to understand that grits don't line up with or against any physical or metaphorical boundaries or borders. Though they have roots in the South, they're enjoyed in many other parts of the world. They make their way north and push far into the Midwest, up to the Northeast, and into the upper reaches of the continent. Indianans have a strong obsession for grits. Italy has polenta, which is a sister to grits. In her book *Victuals*, food writer and Appalachian foodways authority Ronni Lundy wrote about the "Grits Line," saying that it "has been moving steadily north in my lifetime; now even Canadians swear by the pleasures of eating them." (It's true. In 2013, the *Toronto Star* called for Canadians to try their grits drizzled with maple syrup, listing a recipe from the restaurant Rose and Sons.)

This book is not about boundaries, though. And it's not just about grits, really. Mostly, it's about people's stories. Like so many foods, grits help people tell their stories. From home cooks to millers, corn farmers to chefs, those who opened up and shared with me their stories about grits divulged more than just talk of food. They spoke of their lives, their feelings, and their beliefs.

As I researched grits, I saw that the dish provided me with a lens through which I could better understand the place I had come to reclaim. There had been a number of big, thorny topics about the South that, upon moving back, I found myself trying to grapple with: the region's tumultuous history; old and new conversations about race; gender and where and how women find their place here; politics, both in government and in relation to food; and the changing culinary culture through which people across the South, including myself, identify themselves. By writing this particular book, about a dish I didn't fully understand, the story of this region has come into focus for me. And so, too, have my feelings about it.

I'd like to note that there is a lot for anyone to say about grits—even if I'd been given years to research the topic, I'd never find an end to the rabbit holes. But these are the stories that spoke to me. They are different from the ones that another person coming from another angle, from another time, place, and cultural background, might have discovered. And some of them are only partially offered here. This book is not going to connect all the dots or paint a complete picture. In fact, I often feel that the research I did for this project raised far more questions than it answered. But with those questions came the joy of discovery—with every story offered, I was introduced to another angle and another viewpoint of the South to consider.

Through grits I've learned a lot about a complicated and complex region and the many people who have shaped—and are still shaping—its story. Some of these stories are hard to tell and uncomfortable. Others give hope for what's to come. All of them offer proof that this region is forever evolving.

So, if you'll indulge me: It's time to go out and buy a bag of stone-ground grits, maybe even sourced from a local mill, if that's available to you. Whatever you find, pour them into a pot at a ratio of four parts water to one part grits. Let them sit for a minute, or an hour, or even better, overnight. Then bring the whole mess to a boil and reduce the heat to low or very low. Stir frequently. Do not let them stick to the sides or the bottom— which means keep stirring. Once you've given them some time (thirty minutes probably won't do it; try forty-five or, better yet, two to three hours), add just a bit of something. Salt. Some cheese. A splash of half-and-half. A bit of coconut milk. Pepper. Butter, of course. Pile them onto a plate and dip your fork in. You will be eating something good, hearty, and life-giving. And hopefully, it will help you find your own story to tell.

A BASIC RECIPE FOR GOOD GRITS

Serves 4

There are so many kinds of grits available today. I would recommend seeking out a good stone-ground variety, preferably from a local or small-batch source. Keep them in your freezer so that they remain fresh. If you want to amp up the flavor a bit, substitute vegetable or chicken stock for the water. This recipe is just a start. Once the grits are cooked, you can add cheese, cream, half-and-half, or coconut milk to add richness and depth of flavor, especially if you're serving them alongside something else.

4 cups water

1 cup old-fashioned stone-ground grits

Salt

Butter

Pepper

Place the water and grits in a medium pot. Add a pinch of salt. Bring to a boil, then immediately reduce the heat to medium-low. Simmer, uncovered, stirring frequently, until smooth and creamy, 35 to 45 minutes. Serve warm with butter, salt, and pepper on the side.

An Introduction
to Grits

I was about six years old when I first experienced the power of grits. There was nothing particularly nostalgic about the moment. It was not one life-altering, memory-striking bite. It did not occur while I was standing at my grandmother's knee while she stirred the pot.

My experience, on the contrary, involved grits as a weapon of mass murder.

We were living in Spartanburg, South Carolina, where, like most other families in our neighborhood, we had a box of instant grits in the pantry. But at least half my family was just not that into them. Occasionally, on weekend mornings, my mother would pull out the box. My sister and I watched, grossed out, giggling, as the piles of white goo solidified, uneaten, on our plates. Meanwhile, my dad slathered butter, salt, and pepper onto his pile and forked them up enthusiastically.

My dad, Kelly, who grew up in Miami, first ate grits while working a part-time job at a small department store in his hometown when he was in college. The store sat above a café, and before he'd head up to his post in the athletics department, where he would set to work assembling bicycles in time to fulfill a crush of Christmas orders, he would stop by the café to fuel up on an employee-discounted breakfast.

This was during the 1960s, a time when most of the grits to be found were produced and packaged by large, industrial cereal makers, like the Quaker Oats Company or Jim Dandy. The varieties ranged from old-fashioned to quick to instant—all were inexpensive and sustaining. Fuel in a box. At this particular Miami department store café, the grits were likely quick or instant—and for my father, they were a lip-smacking source of deep, belly-filling pleasure.

Later, his full-time career as an engineer with DuPont eventually brought our family to Spartanburg. And it was there, in our two-story blue colonial, that we faced a daily onslaught of one of the South's worst perils: pernicious and vile marching red ants. A menace to our house as both a nuisance and an aesthetic mar, these fiery insects were also a physical threat, their bite stinging and welt-producing, with a venom that unleashed an irritating itch for days. Massive and alien-like, the rust-colored red ants of Spartanburg were as muscled and numbered as the Greeks marching on Troy. As they paraded up and down our patio, creating two-lane highways for themselves, they bustled in endless numbers toward the entrance of our screened-in patio, where they had forged some well-worn path to an invisible but steady supply of food.

Dad loathed the red ants. My sister, Shannon, and I would find him standing, hands on hips or fingers scratching forehead, brow furrowed behind thick, rectangular glasses, at the edge of the patio examining the ground for an end to the ant line. It was a fruitless search. He couldn't determine where these ants were headed or what hidden parcels of food they were attracted to. It was just a long, steady column of drones, mounting a full-frontal attack on nothing in particular, breaching the walls of our unguarded home.

One day, motivated by some unknown discovery, Dad grabbed the cardboard container of instant grits from the pantry shelf and marched outside. We trailed close behind, wondering where in Dad's defense plan the grits came into play. With us watching, Dad leaned over and shook out a trail of grits, drawing a meticulous line of white particles between himself and the ants. A wicked smile lit up his face. He stood straight and looked toward us, his six- and eight-year-old girls.

"Now we wait," he announced, and disappeared inside the house. Shannon and I went back to our Barbies and forgot all about it. A few hours later, we heard him open the patio door and step outside.

"Girls!" he shouted. "Come see." Out we scurried as Dad looked proudly down at the patio where the line of ants had once crawled. The ant line was no longer mobile, nor robust. I kneeled down for a closer look and saw the scars of a battlefield.

Ant bodies lay littered left and right. Severed legs and antennae lay ravaged. Many of the tiny body parts were embedded directly into white clumps of the grits, like tiny ant-flecked pieces of popcorn.

My father, dropper of the grit bomb, beamed. As we examined the carnage, he gleefully explained: Whatever life-giving liquid that existed within the ants' bodies, had, upon coming in contact with the instant cereal product, puffed the grits up, stretching their bodies outward until—boom. This would not have occurred were the grits not industrially modified to expand when they hit liquid. Instant grits were the key. Mission accomplished.

I imagined how shocked the ants were with that first encounter eating grits—consuming without thought, and then, moments later, poof! An explosion from the inside out. And yet the ants continued eating, even as the bodies of their comrades morphed into whitish blobs all around them. Surely, ants have no brains, my six-year-old mind said. Surely, if they did, they would have learned. But these were just drones. Machines following orders. Insects following natural law. Until death by instant grits.

After the carnage had been swept away, the ants would eventually return, causing Dad to haul out the box of instant grits once again.

There weren't a lot of grits in my world after that. I would occasionally encounter them at my sleepaway summer camp in the mountains. Camp food being camp food, you ate what looked edible. I remember piling the butter, salt, and pepper onto the white blob, like I'd seen Dad do, in hopes that they would cover up whatever blob-ish flavor the grits might impart, as well as whatever lingering memory of ant carnage remained. Still, all I tasted was a bland, slimy substance that held no trace of corn flavor. Just butter-flavored mush.

Soon, we moved away from Spartanburg and up north to Cleveland, Ohio. Grits and me parted ways for a while.

❊

Since those steamy Spartanburg days, I've seen grits in all forms. The mounds of congealed white, that instant anomaly, were merely a blip on what would become a journey toward understanding what is actually a complex yet comforting dish. I've since learned that not all grits are created equal. There is, in fact, a pretty significant difference between the mass-produced instant, quick, or flavored grits that many, many people (especially in the South) purchase at the grocery store, and the growing segment of artisanal (or handmade) grits, labeled "stone-ground," "cold-milled," or sometimes "water-milled" available today.

The designations are significant in that they not only tell you how the corn is ground, but also indicate how much the corn is manipulated pre- and post-grinding, and also how much flavor they might exude.

Stepping up the ladder of marketing terms, for example, you'll find fewer and fewer "enhancements" made to the corn to produce grits. So instant grits are usually made from mass-produced GMO corn that's been degerminated, bleached, fed through steel rollers to crush the kernels (stripping out most of the natural corn flavor), and combined with chemically produced vitamins and minerals, which provide the chemical composition the grits need to "cook" immediately after coming in contact with liquid, as well as the proper nutritional content required to appease the FDA's labeling laws, and the preservatives to keep the product shelf stable for long periods of time. The patent created by the food engineers who make instant grits includes "polysaccharide gum, and an emulsifier selected from the group polyoxyethylene sorbitan monostearate, polyoxyethylene sorbitan mono-oleate, glyceryl monostearate, and a mixture of monoglycerides and diglycerides of edible fats, oils, and fat-forming fatty acids." Which—to me, anyway—reads as painfully as swallowing a mouthful of those instant grits I ate as a kid.

Quick grits are manufactured in a similar fashion to instant grits, but the granules are coarser, and while they do have a similar chemical composition for preservatives and nutrition, they're altered slightly so that instead of cooking instantly, they are "fully cooked" in about five minutes.

At the other end of the spectrum, stone-ground grits, which are often an artisanal or small-batch product these days, are typically dried kernels of corn that are ground between two stones, instead of being pushed through steel roller mills. (Stones produce less heat than steel, thereby retaining more flavor in the final product.) After being crushed between stones, the corn is sifted to remove the germ (but not always) before being bagged—no nutritional additives or flavor enhancers are used. (I use the term *bagged* intentionally because most artisanal grits found these days are sold in paper or cloth bags rather than boxes.)

The term "cold milling" adds another step to the process, since the corn kernels are chilled and then milled at colder temperatures, which further helps retain the natural flavor of the corn. Both methods—cold milling and stone grinding—usually result in grits far more flavorful than those that are industrially produced.

Some Southerners also toss around the term *hominy grits*—

these are mostly seen on menus or in recipes, and predominately in the Lowcountry of South Carolina, specifically around Charleston. But it's a confusing and oftentimes misused term. Hominy is made with a processing technique called nixtamalization, wherein corn kernels are soaked in a solution of water and lye—long ago it was wood or plant ash—to remove the outer skin of the kernel. That nixtamalized product, called hominy, can be dried and then ground, making a product called hominy grits. But that process isn't commonly used these days, especially for commercially produced grits. (We'll get into where and when hominy grits are produced a little further along.) For primer purposes, it's good to note that both grits and hominy can be considered "grits." But only hominy can be hominy. Follow?

Yet another point of confusion simmers around the similarities and differences between grits and polenta. Theoretically, grits and polenta are the same thing: ground corn cooked into a porridge. But, technically, polenta and grits differ in several ways, including in the type of corn used to produce the ground product, as well as in the way they have traditionally been milled. Grits are typically produced using dent corn, while polenta is traditionally produced from flint corn. These two varieties differ in their hardness—flint kernels are firmer and rounded on top; dent kernels are softer and have a shallow dent in the top of the kernel. It was flint corns sourced from the Caribbean that Italians started cultivating, grinding, and cooking into porridge around 1500. And although the dish was originally a simple cornmeal mush that could be made from any corn milled to any coarseness, the Italians eventually improved and defined polenta through a technique called reduction milling, where the kernels are ground into large granules and then passed through the mill another time, and then another—the slow process produces less heat than standard single-process milling, and the reduction in heat helps maintain the flint corn's flavor and allows a miller to get the coarseness down to precisely the granule size they want. And, because flint kernels are firmer than dent, cooked polenta firms up into a sturdier porridge with a more defined toothiness than grits.[1] Today, very few producers outside of Italy stick to these guidelines—which only adds further confusion to the differentiation between the two products.

All of that is to say, grits are just corn. Not the sweet eating corn that you find at summer roadside stands, but rather a variety of soft dent corn, which has a high starch content. That starch makes it a product that's ideal for grinding and boiling down. These corns can be found in a multitude of colors—the most popular are white and yellow, but you can also find blue and red varieties, as well as a rainbow of heirloom varieties, from golden orange to deep purple.

Arguments abound on which color corn produces the "best" grits. In certain parts of the South, yellow corn is also viewed as feed corn—"only good for the animals," some might say. In those places, white corn grits are the dominant preference. Other parts of the South view white corn as looking too similar to instant, so those areas prefer yellow corn grits. (I say "areas," but preferences can vary from household to household.) Some say white corn is sweeter; others argue that yellow corn offers more texture. Starch content between different varieties of corn can vary widely, which will affect the cooking time and ultimate flavor of the finished dish. In truth, it all comes down to personal preference.

Grits tend to be a Southern thing. Yes, grits are consumed and found in stores and on menus all over the country and well beyond—the ever-moving "Grits Line," as food writer and author Ronni Lundy calls it. But in the multistate region that spans from Virginia to Texas, there is a passion and love for grits that is prominent and well-known. Grits are the official prepared food of Georgia. The town of St. George, South Carolina, claims to be the highest per capita consumer of grits in the world. (They have not been challenged on this.) Though the point of origin for grits is not in the South, the region can claim notoriety for the proliferation of the dish.

Not only are they mostly eaten by Southerners, they are beloved by Southerners of every stripe: wealthy, poor, black, white, brown, young, old, big, and small. Grits are an equalizing staple—prepared in every style and class of kitchen. And that tradition has endured for multiple centuries. Not every Southerner favors them, of course. Texturally, they can turn people off. (Especially when poured from a packet and cooked in less than a minute.) But for many, it's been written that if grits aren't on the plate, the sun won't shine.

※

Decades after the ant annihilation, I was reintroduced to grits while falling in love with my husband, Dave, who was raised in Knoxville, Tennessee. On my first visit to his hometown, I got to know his mom, Becky, who welcomed me in a number of ways, including the family tradition of a big weekend breakfast. We sat down to plates of eggs, bacon, biscuits, toast, and grits. Seated at Becky's wide dining room table, I spooned a pile of grits onto my plate, wondering whether these would taste as bland as the ones I remembered from my youth. I sliced a pat of butter from the butter plate and laid it over the grits. The yellow mass melted lazily down the edge of the pile. I added a bit of salt and a grind of pepper and then pushed the tines of my fork through the mix, giving the butter a valley to sink into. I took a bite and felt surprise at the nutty flavor coating my tongue. I felt the individual granules pop against my teeth. More than just corn, I picked up on something earthy but also sweet. I was overcome with how rich and satisfying these grits tasted. The pile didn't coagulate on my plate, but rather spread slightly, mixing with my scrambled eggs into a sunshine-colored heap. I scooped up another forkful, this time using the corner of a biscuit to push the grits and eggs together. Taking the whole bite down, biscuit and all, I looked at Becky and grinned—not just because I wanted to please her (though I did), but because something so simple, that she had taken time to prepare, had been so deeply pleasing to me.

That reintroduction to grits started me on an odyssey. Since that meal, and those days when instant grits were all I knew, I've tasted stone-ground grits pooled in broth with a poached egg on top, and also crisply fried into snack-size cakes; I've eaten them mounded in a bowl as a vessel for shrimp; I've tried quick grits that coated an entire plate and were scattered with bits of bacon and cheese; I've sopped up grits served hot and creamy at a Waffle House. Each offered a new opportunity for texture and color— in some instances a blank canvas upon which brushstrokes of bright flavor had been applied.

Although grits are probably most frequently eaten on their own, topped with butter, or mixed with cheese, they've lately been taken into consideration more frequently for their blank canvas appeal, especially by chefs, bloggers, and food magazine editors. Yes, there's flavor to be found in a pile of grits—but, like rice or pasta, they can also be a base for any number of toppings or items mixed in.

There may no longer be a line defining where grits are eaten, but there most certainly is when it comes to what they are eaten with. Twitter feeds and online comment sections regularly heat up with arguments about whether one should or should not put sugar or other sweeteners in their grits. Deep into the pages of any number of Southern cookbooks, the argument arises over whether one should "gussy up" a pile of grits. The late Edna Lewis, a country cook from Virginia who went on to become a well-known restaurant owner and cookbook author, noted that "People should really leave grits alone." Decades later, the Charleston-based cookbook authors and brothers Matt and Ted Lee professed their excitement over trying grits laced with a funky Clemson blue cheese in their book *The Lee Bros. Southern Cookbook*.

It was a "gussied up" version of the dish, discovered at Sean Brock's restaurant Husk Nashville, that further propelled me on my own grits journey. Sean sat at the crest of what had become a tidal wave of "Southern food as trend" that had washed over the food world since he'd opened his New Southern restaurant Husk Charleston in 2010. Announcing that if the ingredient didn't come from the South, "it's not coming through the door," he built himself into a missionary, bent on celebrating and honoring the foods of his native region. Eventually, he opened a second Husk location in Nashville, where the menu focused on the produce and proteins of the upper South. It was there that I was introduced to a dish called A Plate of Southern Vegetables, which was anchored by a bowl of grits.

During an interview in 2015, Sean professed to me that he had an obsession with vegetables—his entire left arm is tattooed with them. I'd called him for a magazine article about how chefs were putting vegetables at the center of the plate; I wanted more details about his Southern vegetable plate. On it, he included four or five components, all vegetable-driven and each crafted with the same treatment he applied to his protein dishes.

The menu item was a storytelling device, Sean explained. "Vegetables and their varieties can be very regionally specific and cooking with ingredients that grow right around you helps tell the story of that region," he said. Between his two restaurants, one on the coast of South Carolina, the other in landlocked Tennessee, the variety ranged dramatically. "The vegetable plate is a way to explore the area right around us which, at different times of the year, even day by day, is changing all the time," he said.

The anchor of the plate was a tall, cone-shaped dish containing grits. Soupy in their consistency, thanks to a brothy base, they sat beneath a poached egg drizzled with herb-infused oil. To eat them, you dipped your spoon into the depths of the cone and pulled up a slurping pile of soft grits, a bit of broth, and a sliver of egg.

I asked Sean about grits during the interview and heard a moan of pleasure on the other end of the line. Then a chuckle. "Get me going on grits and I might not stop," he said. Being on the phone, I couldn't see his expression, but I could read it. A half smile. A light in his eyes.

"Grits," he stated, "are the ultimate expression of *terroir.*"

His comment hung in the air for a minute. My understanding of *terroir*—how an ingredient takes on the flavor characteristics of the specific place where it is grown—was personal. I'd once worked on an oyster farm and learned the term *merroir*, a play on the origin word that applies to ingredients raised in the sea. Oysters pull elements from the seawater they filter and take on those characteristics, so influences like algae, water temperature, and even wind direction can affect final flavor. The same rules applied to land-grown ingredients, including wine grapes and apples, which can channel different flavor profiles depending on where they're grown.

How could grits be a vehicle for *terroir*? What I had been tasting for years—what most people had been tasting since the mass application of steel roller mills and an industrialized agriculture system—was not corn. From a box, the product that gets mixed with water is so stripped of flavor and so "nutritionally enhanced" with additives that the end result couldn't possibly be a vehicle for locational characteristics. Yes, all grits are made from corn, that part I understood. But, so far in my lifetime, I hadn't encountered many examples that could back up Sean's claim.

His comment rattled me. Then it sat with me. And finally it gnawed at me. I wanted to understand his case. Based on my own experiences, it wasn't the grits themselves but rather what you put *on* the grits that gave them flavor. What was it about the corn itself, or even the milling process, that could directly affect the flavor of grits?

With Sean's words in my head, I set out to better understand how grits are produced, and why they could veer so dramatically from the bland instant grits I knew as a child to something that was bursting with corn flavor. I wanted to know what path grits had taken—where they originated, how they became a mass-produced cereal product, and, finally, what brought them into the hands of a chef like Sean, who'd found a way to recapture their true flavor.

Kernels Through Time

Where the Roots of a Dish and a Region Intertwine

Where do grits come from?"

The question was knocking around in my head as I sat down to lunch on the first day of the 2016 Southern Foodways Alliance Fall Symposium in Oxford, Mississippi. The SFA, a group based at the University of Mississippi, was formed to and continuously works toward the mission of documenting and studying the various food cultures of the South, and had been putting on these food-fueled, thought-provoking weekends of discussion, education, and fellowship for more than twenty years. The theme on this particular weekend was "Corn as Symbol, Sustenance, and Problem," so there were talks covering topics like the prehistory of corn and its journey from southern Mexico into the southern reaches of the United States; of corn as the elemental grain of our diet; of corn as a syrupy fuel of the Coke revolution; of African Americans cooking corn bread and making moonshine. Throughout the corn-fueled weekend, I kept wondering how far back in time grits—ground or broken-down corn kernels that are mixed with liquid and cooked until soft—have been in existence.

For lunch, we were inside an event space called the Powerhouse, where many symposia meals took place. Chef Sean Sherman, who went by the moniker the Sioux Chef and whose mission was to educate, serve, and preserve Native American and indigenous foods and preparation techniques, had cooked for us that day.

The food was set on a plain wooden board. Disposable bamboo plates separated five neatly arranged combinations of food. Leaves and herbs, a symbol of the meal's natural elements, accented each dish. On my right, one plate held a pile of shredded, braised meat resting on top of a small mound of purplish-blue grits.

I took a bite of the grits. The meat that mingled with them was cedar-braised bison. Also on the plate were a teosinte flatbread and berried rabbit. The meal was a range of elemental notes, affected little by seasoning or salt. There was subtlety to each bite. Nothing was overdone. It was simple food that forced me to consider each ingredient, but also take note of what wasn't on the plate. In his cooking, Sean avoided the use of any European-introduced ingredients—so no sugar, dairy, flour, beef, pork, or chicken. Instead, he used wild edibles and protein, like fowl and freshwater fish, and the agricultural produce that once filled an indigenous diet, such as corn, sunflowers, and squash.

His grits tasted familiar—simmered slowly in liquid for an

hour or more, they yielded a toothy bite that just barely revealed a bit of their kerneled past. Although these grits were blue, milled from an heirloom Cherokee corn variety that Sean had sourced from Anson Mills, the popular purveyor of milled heirloom grains, they tasted similar to so many versions I'd tasted on other Southern tables.

Few books reference the Native American experience with grits. Yes, there is plenty to be found about the deep indigenous connection with maize, but it's rare to find mention of Native Americans eating or preparing grits specifically. Those references that do exist refer mainly to a moment when British colonists arrived on the shores of Virginia and were greeted by indigenous people holding out steaming bowls of cracked maize. The stories don't go much deeper.

But for me, tasting those purple-blue grits that had been prepared by a member of the Sioux—a tribe located outside of what is now the American South—and by someone who was intent on showcasing the foods of his people, revealed a chasm of untold stories about the direct involvement of Native Americans in the creation of this dish. I found myself asking, *Where are those stories? Is this where grits are from?*

I later called Sean Sherman, looking for clarity. A member of the Oglala Lakota, Sean grew up on Pine Ridge Reservation in South Dakota. Now based in Minneapolis, he'd founded The Sioux Chef as a research project with a mission to showcase indigenous foods, specifically from his own native Dakota and Minnesota territories. The project had grown into a food truck and catering business—at the time of the conference, Sean was raising seed money for a new, all-indigenous restaurant, set to open in the coming year, and he was working on a book. Also, there was a nonprofit called NATIFS, short for North American Traditional Indigenous Food Systems. His hope was to create an educational food hub.

As a child on Pine Ridge Reservation, Sean and his family, like many others, faced poverty. To fight it, his mother went back to school, moving his family off the reservation and into a town in the Black Hills of South Dakota. As his mother studied, Sean spent hours at the college library, digging through books. A studious kid, he enjoyed learning. But he also needed to work. When he was old enough, he took a part-time job in a restaurant kitchen, mostly out of necessity—it was work he could find easily, even at the age of fifteen. He cooked in restaurant kitchens throughout high school, and then again throughout college in order to pay the bills. Something about the work stuck with him, and he moved to Minneapolis to pursue it. By the year 2000, he was working full-time as a chef.

Sean's early career coincided with the first moments of the farm-to-table movement—at the time, only five or six restaurants in Minneapolis touted organic or local ingredients. But he sought them out, choosing to work at the places that were sourcing directly from farmers and ranchers, those who were sowing the early seeds of understanding about how a food system involving grower, chef, and diner could be beneficial for everyone. There, a foundation was already being laid for Sean's understanding of how cooking could accomplish more than providing a meal. Following his curiosity, he started revisiting the foods of his own ancestry and heritage—he even wrote a menu early on made up entirely of indigenous foods and dishes.

Several years into his career, he had a breakthrough. Sitting on a beach in Mexico during an extended vacation, Sean noticed the indigenous community that populated the town where he was staying. The Huichol, he observed, kept their culture very much alive, especially through their foodways. The inspiration propelled him on a new path, with a mission to study and preserve his own heritage.

As he'd learned to do as an inquisitive child during those long days when his mother studied for her degree, Sean turned back to books, analyzing historical texts through a culinary lens. But he quickly learned how little recorded information there was, and how very few books he could find, especially in the form of first-person or first-contact narratives about foods from precolonial history. So he began formulating his own theories, filling the gaps by studying wild foods and plants, teaching himself about botany and the differences to be found in vegetation. As he dug, he formulated an understanding of the ways native people might have accessed the unadulterated outside world. He began to see, in both the past and the present, what it meant to use nature as pharmacy, as grocery store—as everything. Most plants had multiple uses, he learned. And, for centuries, that's what sustained human life.

"It's exciting as a chef to be able to look at indigenous history and see the plant and flavor diversity that exists," he told me. And although, he added, "we have no idea how many varieties we've lost, we have been able to hold on to a few shining examples. Slowly, we're trying to bring these things back."

Sean hadn't eaten grits as a kid, nor had he cooked them often as a chef. But he'd long been playing around with a number of indigenous cooking methods around corn. Nixtamalizing, in particular, was fascinating to him. People were regularly sending him different varieties of corn to experiment with, and he would apply several of the techniques his ancestors might have used, just to see what he could produce. He'd parch, then grind the corn; boil, then grind it; nixtamalize, then grind it. With every application, the corn would act differently, taste different. Like a detective sniffing out a case with few clues, he started to piece together, through these applications, a deeper narrative about how certain varieties of maize had been cultivated and bred for very specific uses.

An Origin Story

Today, we can trace corn back thousands of years, with two prevailing theories on its origins. Corn in its current iteration wasn't something that originally grew in the wild—it was a creation of human hands, a cultivated product. There's evidence that this first occurred in the Central Balsas River valley in southwestern Mexico. One theory suggests that it was a singular event that took place nine or ten thousand years ago when the wild grass teosinte was manipulated by human hands—its seeds selected and crossbred with other vegetation—to produce a version of the kerneled cob we know today. Others argue that it wasn't one moment but more likely a series of continual acts, with many years of agricultural work that employed various methods of cross-pollination and seed saving.

Regardless of the specifics, we know that maize started evolving immediately. With every planting cycle, people were messing with it, breeding new varieties to improve specific qualities. And they were carrying it to new places, sharing it with others, cultivating a different variety based on what suited the landscape or how they were preparing and eating it. These were agriculturalists, traditionally women, who bonded with their plants, creating a relationship with the environment around them—they were capable of understanding what characteristics needed to be strengthened and how to breed for that. They knew how to harness a plant's power and cultivate new varieties, getting different results depending on where it was grown, how well it grew, and what it was being used for. One corn was just right for roasting and popping, another for nixtamalizing, and another for dry grinding.

All the while, during thousands of years of this plant species' evolution, humans were passing along their methods for processing and cooking it, too. The method of making grits, which is as simple as grinding and cooking cornmeal or any other ground vegetable, like wild rice or squash, is a technique that can be found, historically, in just about any indigenous community around the world.

Archeologists studying the region of Central America, where maize likely originated, have uncovered hand stones and milling tools that date back to 8700 BC. So, almost as soon as corn existed, people were grinding it—it's not a stretch to think that they were also putting it in a pot, adding liquid, placing it over heat, and cooking it.

Maize took detours, traveling overseas to Europe via the Spanish, and to Africa, possibly via the Portuguese. From there, it spread farther east and south. We know this because we see corn and cornmeal in cultures all over the planet—there are versions of cornmeal mush, a form of grits, found in cultures throughout the Americas and in southern and central Africa. It goes by names like Indian pudding, *armottes*, mamaliga, *mayi moulen*, *milha*, and, of course, polenta.[2] And each of those bowls of ground-corn nourishment, no matter what they're called, now contain thousands of years' worth of history.

Although corn crossed the ocean, not all of its processing methods went with it. Nixtamalization, for example, which had been passed along for centuries throughout Mesoamerica and North America, wasn't used widely on the corn that reached Europe. The act of soaking corn in wood ash, lye, or lime not only breaks down the kernel, removing the hull, but also adds the key component of alkaline, which alters the protein structure of the corn, increasing the specific protein that delivers niacin to the body—niacin being necessary for us to break down food molecules—as well as calcium, which is delivered to the body through the lime. Whether lime soaking first occurred by evolution or accident, the process allowed corn to become a nutritional staple of the indigenous diet.

Nixtamalization was an overlooked or possibly ignored process in much of Europe, as evidenced by those who experienced corn sickness, a disease that affected the skin, joints, and nervous system. The sickness was termed "pellagra" in Italy in 1771. By that point, polenta had become a dietary staple for many living in the mountainous regions of Italy, mainly peasants. Since corn was cheap and dry-grinding was a simple way to break it down, ground corn porridge was all many ate through winter—but without a protein-improving technique, the corn overwhelmed their system with proteins their bodies couldn't process. Hence, pellagra most often affected the poor. A century later, pellagra became an epidemic in parts of Africa and Egypt; in 1906, it was identified in the United States.

Now, more than a century later, we understand that the reason this nutritional deficiency didn't affect indigenous people, even those consuming large amounts of corn, was because almost every indigenous population that was growing corn, prior to European discovery, was also processing it with an added alkali.

The understanding of corn and the many methods of processing and cooking it was passed along through countless, unnamed indigenous hands—all agriculturists, cooks, and in their own way, nutritionists (again, mostly women). Eventually, maize arrived in the southeastern part of the United States about two thousand years ago.

Although there aren't many written accounts of what was consumed or how dishes were prepared in indigenous diets, grits, or more likely cornmeal mush, do appear in a small number of those. Nancy and Tony Plemmons, members of the Eastern Cherokee tribe in North Carolina, wrote about nixtamal and grits in their book *Cherokee Cooking: From the Mountains and Gardens to the Table*, published in 2000. One of the only food publications in existence that offers a truly Cherokee voice and experience, the self-published, hard-to-find, bound copies recount stories of the foods, ingredients, traditions, rituals, and cooking methods that have been passed down verbally for generations.

There is no recipe for grits in the book, but Nancy relays the stories of making mush from cornmeal. To make the meal, Cherokee women would use a grinding device called a *kanona*, a waist-high, hollowed-out log and a wooden paddle, like a pestle, that had one rounded end. As the pestle came down, the force was enough to crack the stubborn grains. The women would beat dried corn kernels, usually a white variety like Cherokee White Eagle, for thirty or forty minutes to make meal that would range in size from large grits to fine powder. And while they might mix all the meal with hot water in order to cook it down, the mixture would usually be pretty loose, and they wouldn't typically eat it as a porridge. Some might eat cornmeal mush in the morning, but they would also apply a range of other uses to it, like mixing it with chestnut meal to make a chestnut bread; or they would wait until the mixture cooled, then cut it into patties.

Before pigs were introduced to the region by Europeans, the Cherokee would use bear fat or buffalo fat to add heft and protein to the mixture. Or they would cook the cornmeal down with beans to round out the nutritional components of the corn.

Nancy and, for generations before, her ancestors, used nixtamalization to make hominy. They worked outdoors over a live fire using a large, oversize cauldron. There, a tall, wooden paddle was used to stir the corn together with water and wood ash pulled from the remnants of an earlier fire. The process took all day as the corn and ash cooked together. Once the kernel skins had softened, they would start to pop off, revealing the pillowy interior of the corn. The Cherokee might eat the hominy with other proteins, or make a lye dumpling called *di-gu-nv-i*. Once the dumplings were cooked, they could be wrapped in corn husks or hickory leaves and carried as a portable meal.

For centuries before European settlement, these methods were passed along orally, and taught, like the passing of the seed itself, by hand, bringing an early iteration of grits ever closer to the present.

Grits went through several turning points throughout the years. One of the first stands out. Around 1630, as settlers were landing on the shores of Virginia, tribes indigenous to that area offered assistance, exchanging both knowledge and food—here we arrive at the previously mentioned scene of indigenous hands holding bowls of maize out to the new arrivals. This paints a rosy snapshot—but we know that none of this happened easily or without fear. And yet, one can imagine that, like it still does today, the specific act of sharing food eased tensions, perhaps ever so slightly. It also opened up the door to the settlers who would bestow their European name—grist, previously applied to hulled, ground grains, and likely formed from the words *grytt* (for bran) and *greot* (for ground)[3]—on the bowls of cracked, cooked maize set before them.

This moment is critical. This act of translation by the Europeans fundamentally altered the identity of the dish—in an instant, "grits," which the word slowly morphed into, became colonized, recorded, and embedded into mainstream consciousness. This moment launched the official archive of grits: written accounts and trackable moments of a now named dish that could be etched into historical records.

And who got the honor of writing that history?

What's more, through that naming process, grits, the term and the dish, were then permanently tied to what was about to become the southeastern United States. Though that exact preparation of cooking ground corn had already traveled far beyond the region—there's evidence of early forms of stone mills collected from ancient Rome to Asia Minor and Africa—grits, with that specific name, became tied to, and even an identifier of, the American South. So today, if you ask, "Where are grits from?" the answer comes back all wrong.

For Sean Sherman, the story still remains to be told. His role, he explained to me, is to both bring more stories like these to light and to continue the traditions that have been handed to him through the generations.

There was a time, Sean told me, when anthropologists thought for sure that certain Native American cultures were going to be wiped off the map. "People say to me, 'Why haven't these things—these techniques, your style of cooking—why haven't they been done before?' And I'm like, you know, a few hundred years of oppression and genocide will do that, right?"

Establishing Roots

The culinary identity of the South is filled with struggles like this one. Name any dish that is considered Southern, trace it back far enough, and you will unearth stories of theft, slavery, appropriation, and loss—as well as evolution, culture melding, and hope. The story of grits, today a symbol of both comfort and sustenance, is loaded with strife. It began long before the South was even defined, and belonged to far more people than we will likely ever know. And yet, it's also a dish that has evolved. It's adapted with time, and still carries with it that long-lost origin story, as well as the weight of the years that have passed—a weight that increased as grits moved through time, feeding indigenous people and settlers, and later slaves, and big-house masters.

If grits were a baton being relayed through time, Native Americans were the original carriers, but their handoff to the settlers was followed shortly by another handoff, this time to the enslaved Africans who soon inhabited the new American South. For generations of post-settlement arrivals, grits were a cheap, sustaining source of food—especially for the enslaved. As more and more slave-owning settlers arrived, bringing a workforce of Africans with them, the land of the South was put to use cultivating crops for both trade and consumption. The porridge of ground corn, which could be grown and processed in slave gardens and kitchens, continued to play a role as a dietary staple as slavery spread across the South.

In the slave kitchen, corn might have come from rations, or seed collected by hand, or traded with the remaining Native Americans whose own communities were still being systematically descended upon and destroyed. If the slaves were allowed to grow their own food, they raised corn in small plots or kitchen gardens. If they received rations, the corn, which might be given as grits or meal, was part of a few meager staple items provided by the slave owner—identified as the "3 M's" diet, many slaves were given weekly rations of meal, meat, and molasses. If whole kernels could be had, they could be soaked and processed as hominy, or they could be dry-ground by hand, either with a mortar and pestle or a hand mill.[4]

The processing of corn was typically performed by a cook who was most often female. That meant that after working a full day, the enslaved would go back to their cabins and still have to dry-grind kernels of corn by hand; or they'd spend an entire day making hominy over an open fire, which would then be eaten whole and reheated, or dried and ground, and then made into a porridge.

Frederick Douglass, who was born a slave and later freed and became an antislavery activist and writer, tells in his autobiography *Narrative of the Life of Frederick Douglass* how their "food was coarse corn meal boiled. This was called *mush*. It was put into a large wooden tray or trough, and set down upon the ground. The children were then called, like so many pigs, and like so many pigs they would come and devour the mush."[5]

Hominy was an essential part of the diet.[6] The dish was usually simple: hominy, water, a little bit of salt, and a little bit of fatback or salt pork. There was no dairy, but fatback acted as a sort of butter, for lack of a better term. Sometimes, the hominy was dried and cracked to become grits. Other times it was just the hominy itself, served with wild greens or lettuces, and maybe a piece of salted wild-caught fish or salted pork.

Meanwhile, if the slave cooks were also cooking in the big house, they might be making a similar meal for the enslavers they were feeding. So hominy and grits, prepared by black hands, were a part of everyone's diet—in some cases, being eaten from the same pot, making it a shared dish, whether the white slave owners wanted to acknowledge it or not.

Though there were plantations and farms of every size utilizing enslaved workers all over the South, the Lowcountry was known for its large-scale rice plantations, which drove much of the business of slavery in that part of South Carolina and

Georgia in the 1700s. Once settlers came to understand that the difficult grain, which had also been grown along the western coast of Africa from Senegal to Liberia, thrived along that part of coastal South Carolina, slave owners turned to those regions of Africa to purchase slaves who knew how to plant, cultivate, and harvest it. Enslaved West and Central Africans were brought to the region via the Middle Passage, many directly from Sierra Leone, and became the primary laborers of the area's most profitable agricultural product.[7]

The geography of the coastal Carolinas and Georgia is marked by the Sea Islands, a string of barrier islands that stretches from Florida up through North Carolina. These islands, which traditionally housed rice plantations, later became an isolated refuge for freed rice plantation slaves, many of whom stayed there after the Civil War. The isolation of the islands allowed those descendants to preserve their culture.

Now dedicated as the Gullah Geechee Cultural Heritage Corridor, it is an area where the passing along of traditions, food rituals, and historical references has been essential to the preservation of a culture. For many in the Gullah Geechee culture, rice was and is an obvious staple. When slaves worked the rice plantations, they were sometimes given the unsellable dregs of the crop—cracked, imperfect pieces that otherwise would have been discarded. Those pieces would be boiled down and called rice grits.

After the Civil War, families of freed slaves cultivated their own patches of rice. In her book *Vibration Cooking: Or, the Travel Notes of a Geechee Girl*, writer Vertamae Smart-Grosvenor wrote, "I was sixteen years old before I knew that everyone didn't eat rice every day. Us being geechees, we had rice every day." She grew up in Allendale County, slightly southwest of Charleston, eighty miles or so from the coastline, in the 1940s and '50s.

But corn grits were on those kitchen tables, too. African descendent and Gullah community member Sallie Ann Robinson, a cook and food writer born and raised on Daufuskie Island (author Pat Conroy mentioned her in his book about working as a teacher on that island, *The Water Is Wide*), wrote in her own book, *Gulla Home Cooking the Daufuskie Way*: "I grew up eating lots of grits—served soft, thick, chunky, gravied down, and even with a splash of hot bacon grease when there was no butter. Momma said she fed us grits from the time we were born. In our house, grits were the king of the kitchen, and they were the one thing Momma and Pop never let run out."

BJ Dennis, a Charleston chef, caters meals and puts on pop-up dinners to showcase his Gullah Geechee heritage. And while he studies rice and has traced certain varieties of that grain through time, he also recalls his ancestors growing and grinding their own corn grits.

As the Gullah Geechee culture and foodways continue to be written about, discussed, acknowledged, and clarified, we start to see how certain rituals and traditions that were passed from the enslaved to their present-day ancestors—making and eating grits and hominy, included—have influenced and acted as hallmarks of the very roots of Southern cuisine.

A Brief History of Milling

How and where people got their grits evolved quite a bit from the era of pre-settlement to the moment when the first plantations

were established. Once those bowls of cracked maize were introduced to settlers, they quickly became a dietary staple. To crack
the corn settlers used the same techniques they'd been taught, using a hominy block, something similar to the *kanona* used by the
Cherokee, or simply a sturdy piece of wood and a rock pestle. But
once they had their bearings, settlers started to adapt and update
their processes, first with the help of tree limbs—attaching the
"pestle" to a limb, settlers could create a "sweep and mortar" mill.
This style of mill became a popular fixture into the 1700s—so
much so that "sailors traveling along Eastern shores in a heavy
fog could locate land by the 'thump thump thump' of the mills."[8]

Soon settlers started bringing rotary stones over from Europe
to create rudimentary gristmills, which were made up of two
large, heavy, flat, horizontal stones that were cut with correspond-
ing ridges and set atop one another, with the bottom stone set
stationary and the top able to rotate. The stones were attached to
a power source—human, animal, or, in increasing cases, water.
By harnessing water through something called a tub wheel, which
was cut out of a tree trunk, settlers created a primitive type of turbine. They would then connect it via cloth pulleys to a top stone,
which would spin over an immobile bottom stone, creating a
mechanized mill.

The transition to waterpower was a drastic evolutionary
change in how grits could be produced since harnessing water
eliminated the need to use the human body as a power source.
Instead of muscles and bones, these stone-turning devices could
more efficiently break down corn kernels. This also impacted the
role of the miller—instead of women being the primary processors
and hand-grinders of corn and grits, male millers and machine

operators took the reins. Water-powered mills, which were mostly owned and operated by men, thrived across the South for more than a century, even after other modes of power were introduced.

Gristmills were typically run on a toll basis with the miller taking a small amount of the finished meal as payment for using the mill. Oftentimes, the mills were put in place by wealthy landowners or others with financial stature in the community.

In some cases, mills preceded general stores and even courthouses—some communities were founded at the mill, with the charter written there before a courthouse was built. The mill was a gathering place, where peddlers would bring in goods, so it became a source for daily bread, goods, and information. The miller collected and shared information about what was happening two hollers over, how other communities were getting along, and what they were growing. Millers had a reputation for being unscrupulous—often they would toll the meal that they were milling using toll scoops or toll buckets to scoop out the "pay." But some would also put a discharge at the back of the mill stones that would drop a small portion into the basement, meaning they could increase their share of the toll without anybody being the wiser. And the miller usually knew when and where someone was going to be making moonshine—the grain miller and the moonshiner were oftentimes one and the same.

While gristmills thrived across the South, there were also merchant mills, which were used more for commercial production. They mostly existed in New England, with some popping up in the South prior to the Civil War. But it was Oliver Evans, an inventor born in Delaware, best known for his pioneering work on the high-pressure steam engine, who updated the industrial production system in order to create efficiencies in grain grinding. In 1784, he built a system in which several separate machines—conveyors, elevators, scales, and mill—were all automatically powered from the same waterwheel source. Grain would be poured into a spout, carried by conveyors and elevators to a stone-burr mill, then to a separator, or bolter, and then on to a cleaner, eventually getting spouted out as a milled product—all powered by the same water-forced wheel. His was the second US patent ever distributed.

Evans's process was eventually adopted by the flour industry and later replaced by a more up-to-date process in the 1870s, which was then replaced completely with the introduction of steel roller mills in the 1880s. Though Evans's process was mostly used for commercial operations, it could, on a small scale, also be applied to small, water-powered gristmills.

Steel roller milling, which advanced and evolved after the 1880s, became the primary method of grits production in the early twentieth century. Several small mills in Ohio—including one called Quaker Mill Company, which milled oats, and F. Schumacher Milling Company, which milled oats and other products, including corn grits—eventually merged to create the American Cereal Company, which then became the Quaker Oats Company. Jim Dandy, a brand founded in Alabama in 1892 that produced grits at a mill in Kentucky, first trademarked their production of grits and cornmeal in 1923. These two brands, along with Aunt Jemima, have dominated the grits market ever since. And while that huge market share managed to push out many hundreds of small community mills, some of which still exist but don't operate, a handful of holdovers still thrive today.

Into the Modern Day

In Kittrell, North Carolina, down several winding back roads that still hide a few large, antebellum houses, J. Daryl Spencer runs the Buffaloe Milling Company, producer of Water-Ground Style Moss White Grits.

Daryl maintains a molasses drawl that disappears into his chin when he speaks. Inside his office, a pencil sketch shows the mill's original twenty-five-foot waterwheel, which was built around 1850. Originally, a landowner with the surname Hunt built the mill and allowed everyone in the nearby community to use it. Hunt, like many of his day, collected a toll to use the mill.

Although Hunt had built the building and the original waterwheel, it had changed hands several times over the years. Daryl's own grandfather Johnnie Moss purchased the mill in 1950, then leased the business to his son-in-law, Daryl's father. Daryl came to work the mill in the late '70s after a few semesters in college, and in 1989, he purchased the business from his father outright.

Along the way, the operation of the mill transitioned from waterpower to diesel to electric and has grown from two horizontal stone mills to six. Since taking over, Daryl has also expanded the business—there are now more than thirty mill employees, and they make more than a dozen types of corn products, including meal, grits, breading mixes, and even hush puppies.

Today, the millhouse goes through several thousand pounds of corn each week, with grits being a big part of the business. And

Daryl attributes the rising popularity of grits, in part, to the continual operation of his family's mill.

In Midway, Kentucky, another historical, family-owned business, Weisenberger Mills, has been a working grain mill for more than 150 years.

Set a short ways outside of Lexington, just a few miles away from the lush, perfectly manicured acres kept up for the area's famous racehorses, Weisenberger sits on the lip of South Elkhorn Creek. Purchased by Augustus Weisenberger in 1865, it has continually operated as a grain mill and remained in the same family since then. The original building was torn down around 1910, due to a crack in the structure—the building that stands now was built by Augustus's son Philip in 1913. Today, the mill produces wheat flour, cornmeal, and grits and is under the helm of Augustus's great-great-grandson, also named Philip, and Philip's father, Mac.

The current Philip is a youthful fortysomething with a head of thick black hair. He started working at the mill as a teenager, sweeping floors and cleaning out the grain bin, in order to save up some money.

Though the building has been updated over the years, today it shows its age—decades of use as a working mill has given it the patina of experience, with well-worn floor boards and sets of rickety staircases that lead to the upper floors. A fine layer of corn flour now coats the machinery.

The system Weisenberger uses to mill grits involves a steel roller mill; the mill itself is a series of horizontally stacked rollers that are etched with a corrugated surface, which crack the corn kernels as they fall through. The distance between the rollers can be adjusted with a lever, allowing for different size granules depending on the distance that's set. Once the corn is fed through, the cracked kernels are then sent to a separator, set with varying sizes of screens, and sifted to produce grits and cornmeal, with the finest bit left as corn flour. The company also mills wheat flour with an entirely different set of mills that are located on a different floor than the corn mill. The machinery is decades old, with many of the mills, elevator systems, and system mechanisms dating back to Philip's grandfather's time.

The original water turbine still sits under the building. Built to hang just slightly over the edge of the creek, the millhouse contains a false floor toward the back through which a vertical rod juts down into the water. Attached to the rod are large horizontal flaps that act like propellers, gaining momentum as the water rushes past. What now seems rudimentary was once a technological feat that powered all the mechanized operations of the mill for decades.

In the mid-'80s, the Weisenbergers replaced that turbine with a generator, and they've since updated the technology with an even newer one. But, technically, the operation is still water-powered, in a roundabout way. Now the energy that comes in through the generator is sent directly to the utility company, passed through the grid, and comes back to the mill as energy credits. Today, they run the generator long enough to produce about 75 percent of their power. The entire mill is now operated off two water turbines and generators that are connected to the mill's complicated system of mills, belts, elevators, and pulleys.

The original installer of the hydroelectric system, David Brown Kinloch, recently came back to Weisenberger to experiment with a new generation of hydroelectric power. Through a

US Department of Energy grant, Kinloch and the University of Kentucky's Center for Applied Energy Research installed an experimental new system that uses a variable speed generator. The small, demo project has been a huge success—the generator captures about 96 percent more power than the old system.[9]

Today, when Weisenberger does grind corn, they grind about six to eight thousand pounds of it at a time, both white and yellow varieties, mostly for meal. When they mill for grits, which happens about once a week and requires an adjustment of the rollers, they only mill about two thousand pounds.

Although the mill has upgraded some of its technology, the space itself is a step back in time. Up on the second floor, where the air sparkles with a fine, omnipresent powder, several dozen strings hang from the ceiling, each holding a worn-out golf ball. Philip's grandfather installed them half a century ago and they still operate the intricate system of belts that move grain around the building. It's as low-tech as you can get, but has served the employees smoothly and efficiently ever since it was installed. Not much changes at Weisenberger. Even the massive, industrial-scale sewing machine that weaves threads through every bag of milled grains has the heft and simply engineered technology of a bygone era. But that lack of change is what keeps it going—a mill that runs as steadily as the power-supplying creek it sits on.

For Philip, the lack of change and especially the slow pace of innovation took some getting used to. As a twentysomething kid, he'd go crazy trying to convince his grandfather that they needed new products or to upgrade with the times. Today, he understands why his grandfather stuck with the same methods and products they'd always used: They worked.

The one major shift the mill made came around 1990, right before Philip got his start in the business: The family added grits to their product line. Although Philip's grandfather had brought the milling operation and its products into the twentieth century, he was averse to making more changes as he aged. The decision to add grits, though, was unanimous. The company had been getting constant requests from their customers, many of whom were seeing grits appear on more and more menus or popping up in parts of the country they traditionally hadn't, and like many small, family-run mills of the era, Weisenberger jumped at the opportunity. Though grits are not the company's biggest seller, the packaged dried corn product is steadily pumped into the company's white paper bags and shipped out on pallets week after week.

※

Another torch-passing moment for grits, which, along with water-powered milling, carried the processing and distribution of the dish into the twentieth century, was the arrival of the vertical stone mill. The story of grits follows the through-line of manufacturing throughout the South, and the invention of the vertical stone mill assisted in the creation of new and varied types of manufacturing jobs. As the region rebuilt itself after the Civil War, commercial manufacturing took off, and small pocket communities were built and sustained with the production and workforce required to run local mills.

Meadows Mills can claim a role as both creator of those opportunities and preserver of the grits milling tradition. In 1902, William Calloway Meadows, who had fought in the Civil War, created a vertical, portable mill that was suitable for grinding cornmeal, wheat, and other grains. Prior to his invention, most mills used horizontal stones laid flat. Meadows's version turned the stones on their side, producing a vertical system. Encased in a box and attached to a small engine, the vertical version took up less space than larger horizontal machines and soon were joined by additional equipment, including the grits bolter, or separator, which allowed for the product to go from kernel to sifted, ready-to-be-bagged final product with just the flip of a switch. These compact systems made milling grits and other grains accessible on a larger, yet still not industrial, commercial scale.

Calloway's son, Bob Meadows, would eventually improve on the design, creating an iron-framed corn mill. Meadows Mills went on to produce saw and hammer mills as well as cornmeal bolters, those automated sifting machines—originally all of these were produced with wooden casings but were upgraded to all-steel casings around 1950.

Located in North Wilkesboro, North Carolina, at the southern end of Appalachia, Meadows Mills is now co-owned by Bob Hege, who has handed most of the running of the operation on to his son, Brian. Bob, one of five brothers, grew up on his family's nearby fourth-generation dairy farm. Though his brothers all stayed on the farm, Bob went to school and later took a job with Duke Energy. After working in agricultural sales for several years, he heard about Meadows Mills coming up for sale. The manufactory, which had switched hands and expanded with the purchase of other manufacturing businesses along the way, also produced farming equipment, and Bob was familiar with their products. In October 1990, he and partner John Davis purchased the business for just north of a million dollars and have been running it ever since.

Since the start of Meadows more than a century ago, the town of North Wilkesboro has seen plenty of change. Once the third-largest city in North Carolina, the population topped out at sixty-five thousand people. But tough times hit after a flood in 1916, followed by another in 1940—about a third of the population left after each one. It was a thriving center of both furniture and textile manufacturing—both industries that have leveled off across the country, or nearly disappeared, thanks to international competition. The Meadows Mills manufacturing facility, which at one point employed one thousand people and was spread out over five buildings, has dwindled to one warehouse and thirty-eight employees. The employees who fill the space range from a few guys in their early twenties to an employee who's been with Meadows Mills for forty-five years.

The current home of Meadows Mills is the length of a football field and still manufactures farming equipment as well as new grain mills—they've produced more than twenty-seven thousand since the inception of the business and still have records of almost every single product serial number. The product line today ranges from a small, home-friendly 8-inch stone mill to 12- and 16-inch mills and on up to mills that are 42 inches and larger.

At the very back of the building sits the maintenance and repairs department, where a handful of skilled laborers have the knowledge to fix overused stones, or restore and rebuild recovered machines that people have found hidden away. Brian Hege has become especially interested in the recovery of old Meadows Mills machines—he spends time scanning eBay and other sale sites where the machines are often being sold as junk or unused antiques. He'll purchase them for a low price and have them brought to the warehouse, where the team can restore and repair them, re-dress the stones, and clean up the machines, which Meadows can then resell. The company doesn't necessarily see a profit with these restorations, but for Brian, it's more important that the machines are put back to use rather than rusting away.

Mostly, the new mills made by Meadows today are going to commercial bakeries or companies producing canned goods. The restored pieces, on the other hand, usually go to what Brian calls the "engine-heads," as well as a rising number of distillers. The company owes a lot of thanks to the moonshining industry, in fact—the process of distilling at home requires that moonshiners grind their own corn, and Meadows Mills has long been one of the most popular products for getting that done.

Whether producing grits in the edible or drinkable form, or grinding any number of other grains or ingredients, the machines produced by Meadows have provided generations of people around the world with an efficient method for breaking down food into a consumable form. But they've also provided countless skilled laborers, both those who have built, and those who have gone on to run these machines, the opportunity of a career, one that not only feeds families, but also communities.

As Bob Hege and Brian Hege continue their work at Meadows Mills, they're providing more machines and, therefore, more job opportunities. They're continuing an American-manufactured product line, and preserving one tiny little corner of this country's long manufacturing history. They're also building an insurance policy, especially with their work on restoring those older machines, which in turn maps out a future for the industry. Their form of stewardship makes the production of small-batch, stone-ground grits (as well as wheat and meal and liquor) possible, and guarantees the tradition for generations to come.

An Eye Toward the Future

Along with upgrades to the milling process came upgrades in agriculture. As grits leapt through time, the production methods changed, and so too did the corn that was used to make grits. Thanks to technology, what had been a hand-produced, stone-milled product brimming with flavor prior to the turn of the century soon became a mass-produced, flavorless breakfast product found in boxes on grocery store shelves. The arrival of quick grits, "flavored" grits, and instant grits—an invention developed by Quaker in the 1960s—though revolutionary for home cooks, also took grits back several steps.

Once corn became a commodity crop in the United States, various applications for the grain became widespread—from animal feed to fuel to cereal. Seed producers started working in a lab instead of a field, pushing varieties of corn into new territory by optimizing seeds to account for higher yields and immunity to pests, rather than for flavor or usage. Around this time, grits started to lose their flavor. Corn varieties like Cherokee White Eagle or Carolina Gourdseed, which had once produced grits that had a depth of flavor and color, were not high yielding or good for large-scale production, and therefore were no longer grown by commercial farmers—instead, those farmers put their land to use planting generic, hybridized corn varieties, which were then purchased by large cereal makers to be milled. When those high-starch, low-sugar corn kernels were processed, de-germinated, and passed through high-heat-producing steel mill rollers, the end result became a dry mound of flavorless corn bits.

Heirloom varieties persisted, though, thanks to small-plot growers who would pass seeds along or trade them with neighbors, but they were hard to come by and often tucked away in hidden fields so they wouldn't cross-pollinate with the large-scale production crops. Meanwhile, a small number of water-powered mills continued to operate across the South, despite the competition put forth by large cereal makers.

In the 1990s, a man named Glenn Roberts came to the realization that the historical flavors of certain grains had been lost or were on the verge of disappearing—and that very few growers or millers were working to preserve those grains. So he found a way to make that his mission.

Glenn's story and the story of Anson Mills have been widely published. Glenn, an expert in historical architectural restoration who was raised in California by a mother from Edisto Island, South Carolina, started thinking seriously about lost grains after attempting to host a historical dinner on a restored Charleston property and being faced with a bag of Carolina Gold Rice—the accurate grain of the time period and a variety available from only one source—that arrived full of weevils.

Since setting out on his quest to put certain heirloom and antebellum grains into production in the 1990s, Glenn has become a force in the Southern food community—and it all unfolds from an unmarked Columbia, South Carolina, facility.

Columbia, thanks in part to Glenn, has become an epicenter

for grits production. Dubbed the "secret grits capital of the world" by a journalist writing for the *Free Times* in 2011, the city has received a reputation as a mill town recently for Glenn's work—but long before he came into the picture, there was Adluh Flour Mills, started around 1900, which still stands and operates at the center of town today. The tall concrete block that houses Adluh rises above Gervais Street, a few blocks away from Anson. Red block letters stretch across the graying white building, a beacon of historical record in a town that's been modernized with beer gardens and high-end restaurants. At night, a neon sign blinks the name "Adluh" over the hotels and shops that surround it.

For its first twenty years, Adluh was operated by a single family and only milled corn. It was taken over by the Allen family in the mid-1920s; they turned it into a flour mill but continued to mill a small amount of grits as well. A 1946 Mill-O-Matic is still in operation in the original mill building—but the company only uses it to grind grits and meal for local restaurants and to supply their own online store, where they sell stone-ground white and yellow grits by the pound.

Today, Adluh mostly produces flour for large wholesale accounts. They also license their name to a small mill in North Carolina that produces cornmeal, which can still be found on grocery store shelves in many parts of the South.

Adluh's very existence helped provide a staging ground for Glenn, who created Anson with a crop of Carolina Gourdseed corn, an old mill, and a few big ideas. Nearly two decades later, Anson, which sits in the heart of this Southern town, has had a hand in training a small army of talented millers, instilling them with a heightened knowledge for grits, for heirloom grains, and for the machines.

For a better sense of how Anson operates, I visited the humble Columbia facility, where I met with the operation's founder, who was, like always, in a state of constant motion.

"Nobody is working in the live kitchen, nobody even *defines* it," Glenn stated as we sat across from each other in his cluttered office. His eyebrows lifted over his blue-gray eyes, and his feet pitter-pattered between thoughts. A swoop of silver hair just barely grazed his eyes. He hunkered forward, as if bringing me in for a secret.

"We based this company on the concept of the live kitchen," he said. "Know what that is? It's like, why would you mill corn right out of the field? Because it tastes different than it does when it goes dormant, right?"

His chair was wedged between two desks, one covered with a two-foot-high stack of cookbooks, and a shelf that held a microwave. On another shelf, sitting atop a cutting board, there were small piles and clear plastic baggies full of corn kernels and grains of rice—telltale evidence of his addiction.

He fidgeted with his thumb as he spoke. Somewhere within his coded lecture, there was a message. He had learned and forgotten more about grits culture than most—he was operating on a different plane. Fresh milling holds a key to life, he seemed to say. And his goal was to guide people there, on a path toward unlocking some giant cabinet of truth.

Even before eating Sean Sherman's blue grits, which he'd sourced from Anson Mills, I'd read countless profiles and portraits of Glenn, who was at the helm of this modern-day mill. Chefs have referred to this purveyor of heirloom grains as brilliant, and have painted him as a tireless researcher, experimenter, and explorer, as well as a savior of flavor itself. For several decades, Glenn's drive has been to discover, grow, and distribute varieties of corn, rice, and other grains that have nearly disappeared—all in an effort to reintroduce flavor. By sharing those grains with chefs—in the United States and, increasingly, beyond—he's ensured a market for even the most obscure, ancient varieties.

Glenn's interest in lost flavors came after the realization that many varieties of these grains no longer existed, wiped out by industrialization and modern agriculture. So hell-bent on recapturing not just lost seeds and milling styles, but taste, Glenn sought out bootlegging camps, traipsing into hidden cornfields spread throughout the hollers of Appalachia, to gather corn seeds. He'd discovered that it was in the backwoods, at unseen, family-run bootlegger operations, where some varieties of dent corn and flint corn were being preserved. These families were grinding the corn with small, engine-powered mills in order to make whiskey mash. But Glenn knew these varieties also made good grits. There's no clear telling of where he found his first batch of seed or from whom—for obvious reasons, he's protective of that particular group and place—but he found them, collected their seeds, and set to work revitalizing the stock, one crop at a time.

Since starting Anson in 1998, Glenn has worked with farmers all over the country, handing out corn like a modern-day Johnny Appleseed in order to repopulate specific varieties. Meanwhile, he also supplies the final product—grits, but also cornmeal, polenta, and rice and rice grits—to the world's best chefs with a product that is unmatched in flavor, in order, he explains, to move a cuisine "vigorously and robustly forward." All of it, he believes, will help him create his vision of the live kitchen.

Thomas Keller was one of the first to discover Anson's products. Glenn originally tried to sell him grits, but Keller insisted they wouldn't fly at his temple of haute cuisine, The French Laundry. Instead, he requested Glenn's polenta, which was made in a traditional Italian style from revived ancient varieties of flint corn (grits, remember, are made with dent corn).

The key in either case, Glenn discovered, was chilling the corn before it was milled—what he calls cryogenic, or cold, milling—and also using different mill settings for the two products. After the milling process, both the grits and the polenta were sifted over screens, which allowed for consistency in the particles. The germ, which had been crushed with the rest of the kernel, was where the flavor lived. It was then released when the grits or polenta were cooked slowly over low heat. There are many stories of chefs discovering unlocked flavors after mindfully stirring a pot of Glenn's grits. Sean Brock, for one, learned to taste *terroir* in grits thanks to Glenn's teachings.

In the twenty years he's been in operation, Glenn's star has risen to a point that he's become almost uncomfortable with—during my visit, he went off on a tangent about his desire to "unbrand" Anson Mills. But that success has also provided him with the means to continue his work and push in new directions. Though he claims to be making nearly no profit, the modern-day grits revivalist now sells his Antebellum Coarse White Grits at wholesale to chefs for almost $4 per pound; polenta goes for nearly $7 a pound. Retail customers pay $6 for 12 ounces.

Comprised of a few unmarked, purposefully nondescript warehouses that sit behind a car wash, Anson's world headquarters is where all the company's fresh milling takes place. The buildings house a few milling rooms, a seed house full of walk-in refrigerators, and cluttered offices. This is Glenn's safe harbor, where those seeking him are intentionally guided off track. He keeps it derelict for a reason: His money all goes into seed saving.

When we met, Glenn spoke in a quick staccato, occasionally opening up to allow for conversation, posing questions, with a punctuating "right?" after just about every sentence. His voice filled the room, booming when he was on a good thread, but pulling back into a softer tone when his curiosity took over, as though the volume of his tenor fell in sync with his brain waves. Much like how he lives his life, Glenn doesn't sit for long—he and I were up on our feet after about twenty minutes, moving toward a storage room where he wanted to show me a hand quern he'd found. He's on planes—to speaking gigs, to farms, to his other home in Martha's Vineyard—more than he's not.

All the while, he talked. He had questions he wanted to ask. Had I gotten to the topic of rice grits? Will I cover that? Probably not, he answered for me. How about the "prepared" word for grits and "the difference between whole hominy"? He rolled right past my answers to make his own points about each.

We walked toward the unmarked milling house and Glenn pointed at a long, seemingly dilapidated building. "This nasty facility? We've spent literally hundreds of thousands of dollars trying to keep it as ugly as possible," he said, giggling. Inside, massive walk-in coolers, kept at 45 degrees, stored hundreds of types of seeds, he explained, for both production and research. Another hundred or so varieties filled the half-ton freezers at the end of a building—over there, he gestured. Between Texas and Martha's Vineyard, there were four research farms, plus other seed houses with "critical reserve everywhere. We replicate, replicate, replicate," he explained. They also store seed at an off-the-grid seed vault near Charleston. "We provide seed pro bono to farmers and we don't monetize it at any level, ever," he added, insisting that he doesn't actually sell seed. "Essentially, we're a not-for-profit," he stated with a half grin. "And my accountant is pretty much convinced of that."

Guiding me up a metal staircase, he led me into the mill building through a loading dock doorway. The light was dim and the room was cool, almost chilly. One part of the room was taken up by pallets piled with white bags full of grain, and every few feet there stood another piece of equipment. Glenn pointed to one, a large mill set on a red wooden base with a dust-covered funnel spout and a small industrial fan set on one side. "That's from the 1920s—we use it all the time," he said. Beside it sat a separator, also called an eccentric sifter, which was a white vertical box made up of nine screens stacked atop one another.

"Smell that?" he asked, eyes flashing. "Can you tell what variety of maize that is?" I shook my head, bewildered. "Me neither," he snorted. And then: "Is that Jarvis? Smells like it to me." He motioned toward someone hidden from view. "He's roasting corn over there. And Jarvis is one of those weird grits corns, with enough native genetics that it's showing its purpose," he said. There were different techniques for making grits, he intoned, like nixtamalization and what he called acido basilisk, or sour grits. And then there was the alcohol-ferment grits. "One method natives used was to create a vinegar out of grape juice, letting it sit in the sun to create a very high Brix, or sugar content, and then pouring it over dry-ground grits. The pH in the liquid would actually change the color and flavor profile of the corn," he explained. "Everyone should be doing this, and no one is," he added, matter-of-factly.

But getting back to Jarvis. "It's a Quaker corn. It's also an Amish corn, and a Mennonite corn. But it was actually the Moravians who brought it out of the Native American culture of Winston-Salem," he marveled. "So Jarvis was a Winston-Salem-specific heirloom corn, and the grits from it are not spectacular. They're good, but they're not great. But when you parch it, that aroma explodes."

I sniffed the air again and caught a bright, sweet nuttiness wafting past, like the air you cut through while passing by a bakery on a city sidewalk. Underneath the aromatics were hints of gasoline and must.

We walked toward one end of the room, and as Glenn opened a door, the loud whir of something resembling an airplane engine erupted. Suddenly, Glenn's words were washed away in an ocean of noise. A few guys wearing full-body coveralls and masks over their faces worked alongside the tall, vibrating mechanics of an electric-powered mill. One guy, wearing massive yellow headphones hitched to one side of his head, only partly protecting his ears, stood toward the loading end, pouring grain into a wide, funnel-like top. The grains fell downward, into the stone-on-stone mill. With the help of blowers and fans, the milled product then shot upward through a series of pipes and over into a tall, rectangular separator, which housed several vertical screens that caught the grain after it was milled. The box was gyrating, like it was wearing a Hula-Hoop, shimmying the grains down from one screen to the next, separating the particles so that the larger pieces stayed on the top screens with the finer dust falling toward the screen below. Another tube then carried the separated, milled grain into a bin, while yet another evacuated the unwanted chaff into a cloth-covered receptacle. A layer of white powder clung to the machines.

All of it, I realized as we made our way around the buzzing room, was Glenn's version of a modern-day live kitchen—a space where the food remains alive even as it's processed and packaged for distribution. There was a very palpable energy inside that space, and Glenn's crew moved with a sense of urgency—as though the grains, just harvested, needed to be moved along immediately so they remained full of flavor.

To one side, I saw a miniature laboratory, where a few guys, also masked, stood over large metal bowls, hand-sifting milled grits, separating the meal with round metal-rimmed screens into industrial-size metal bowls. The men looked just like line cooks I'd seen in fine-dining kitchens, heads down close to the bowls, eyes lasering in on the task at hand. Lined up in front of them, tall, clear pitchers of grain sat waiting to be sifted.

Away from the milling space, in another part of the room, a row of four basic white kitchen ovens were lined up beside one another on a platform—the source of the smell of the roasting Jarvis. Tall beige bins sat around them—I tried to read the labels and could see that all contained some variety of rice or corn that was soon to be milled.

Glenn, who'd been nattering away as I took in the scene,

stepped closer to shout into my ear the names of the guys in the room. "That's Kevin, he's been with us forever. Adam, he's over here, he graduated college, then took two years off and decided to study macro greens. Mike, Daryl, Ephraim, Allen—this guy's a retired marine."

These were the worker bees in Glenn's hive, dutifully manning the mills each day (and probably at night, too) to produce the four hundred styles of product Anson peddled to chefs and consumers. Every order—some that required corn that was grown, nixtamalized, or parched to get the flavor of the granules just so—came from the hands of this team, from grain bin to mill, hand-sifted, hand-collected, hand-packaged. All Glenn's talk and knowledge and research—live kitchens, heirloom seeds, hand querns—was only the outer shell of the Anson hive, I realized. Inside, the worker bees bustled. This was where it all happened, day in and day out—all in pursuit of introducing the world to a better form of grits.

I wasn't shown all of it, of course. Anson's chillers were, for proprietary reasons, tucked away, shielded from the potentially idea-stealing gaze of a visitor yielding a tape recorder and camera. I was never fully clued in on how, when, or where the cold part of the cryogenic milling process came into play, but the way Glenn spoke about it, the very act of keeping the grains chilled throughout the milling process was what gave his product its magic.

I realized that while on the outside, Glenn's operation looked like any small food-manufacturing operation, it was, in fact, a pumping heart, giving life to an entire body of work. And that's what Anson has become—a body of work that, like a history book, helps carry a story about the past. Though the story was written from the perspective of one person's lens—a person who was, regardless of his claims, making at least some form of profit on the past—that story has helped clarify a segment of our history by bringing it viscerally into the modern day. Through Anson's grains, we can now taste something very similar to, if not exactly like, grains that might have been eaten centuries before. Though the growing process, production methods, and even cooking processes have been updated and modernized, the grains themselves have become a vessel through which we can explore the history of the South.

Grits on the Move

While Glenn's work has been lauded, and rightfully so, for bringing flavorful grits into so many restaurant kitchens, it was the work of many more before him that guided us into the present grits moment.

After the Civil War, grits started making their way north, thanks mostly to the participants of the Great Migration—the former enslaved African Americans and their ancestors who started moving northward after the war in search of a better life and better opportunity. Whether it was to Chicago for manufacturing or the Midwest for the prospect of land, Southerners migrated, and the foods of the South moved with them.

In the decades directly after the Civil War, recipes for grits started appearing in national print. In 1891, *Ladies' Home Journal* listed a recipe for breakfast shrimps, showing the reader how after boiling the shrimp, "a wrench of the head, a twist of the tail" would slip the meat out easily and firm. They were to be placed on a bed of hominy grits.

It wasn't long before grits started appearing in restaurants outside of the South, too. Izola's Family Dining opened on Chicago's South Side in 1940, serving up cheese grits, fried chicken, and grilled liver with bacon. In the 1960s, South Carolina native Sylvia Woods purchased the Harlem café where she was working as a waitress and renamed it Sylvia's Restaurant, where she offered grits for breakfast and dinner.

Though it might have been one of just a few spots in New York serving grits at the time, Sylvia's, which is still open despite the passing of its namesake owner, has been joined by dozens of grit-slinging restaurants. Today's New York is heavily peppered with transplanted Southerners, who make their way to the ten-year-old throwback Williamsburg joint Pies 'n' Thighs for fish and grits, or to the elevated Southern spot Root & Bone for a side of stone-ground grits mixed with pimento cheese and grilled corn.

In 2013, the Lee brothers, Matt and Ted, who were dividing their time between Charleston and New York, ranked New York's best shrimp and grits for *New York Magazine*. They awarded four and a half out of five stars to Mama Joy's for the "aggressively seasoned" grits, noting that they'd been sourced from Georgia's Logan Turnpike Mill. They firmly critiqued most of the other spots on the list—one got demerits for adding honey and others simply for the quality of their grits.

Andrew Knowlton, once deputy editor at *Bon Appétit*, has long been vocal about his Southern roots and has written prolifically about the institutions he holds dear—he once wrote about working a 24-hour shift at a Waffle House, simply because of his deeply held appreciation for the Southern chain. When I reached out to ask where he ate his grits in New York, he responded that his current favorite place to eat them was inside the Condé Nast cafeteria. After the curmudgeonly food editor complained for years about the lack of good grits to be found, the cafeteria cooks broke down and started making them for the Georgia transplant.

In my own life, ever since meeting Dave, I kept an eye out for grits in the northeast. In Boston in the early 2000s, we could occasionally find grits on the menu at some Southern-inspired joints, like the now closed Hungry Mother, named for the Virginia state park near which its chef, Barry Maiden, grew up. His skillet chicken with creamy grits called to us on many frigid New England nights. Nearby, a born-and-bred Bostonian, chef Tony Maws, managed to work magic in the form of a dessert of creamy white corn grits, which he topped with dried fruit compote, hazelnuts, and a perfectly smooth quenelle of ice cream.

In 2016, we traveled to Napa and Sonoma for a long-awaited celebration of our tenth anniversary. To cap off the trip, we enjoyed a meal at Meadowood, a dreamy resort with a Michelin-starred restaurant, where chef Christopher Kostow puts forth a painstaking amount of work to produce visually arresting dishes from pristine ingredients. We feasted on cucumber seed risotto with caviar and "dry coastal grasses," and grilled duck with a rhubarb mustard "fudge." At the end of the meal, we were invited to take a tour of the kitchen, a tradition in some Michelin-starred establishments. As we passed through the gleaming-white, nearly silent space, which felt more like a lab than a bustling restaurant kitchen, I peeked at some of the containers lined up along a shelf and saw that one clear tube was filled with a ground coarse yellow cornmeal that looked strikingly similar to dry-ground grits. The label read "Geechie Boy," which is the name of a grits miller on Edisto Island, South Carolina. Grits, it seemed, had long ago found their way to the West Coast and into this temple of haute cuisine.

❊

From their origins in indigenous cultures to their travels throughout the world, grits trace their lineage far beyond the South. And yet as soon as the dish became tied to the American South, its existence both helped create and was transformed by the same things that have come to define the region. Like so many Southern foods, as grits traveled and transformed, they carried the region's stories with them. The most significant of those stories came from the people who carried the dish from one generation to the next—and those stories, though not often told, most frequently came from people of color.

Red, Brown, Yellow, and White

Blurring Lines Between the Color of Grits

I n 2016, during the filming of a reality television cooking competition, pop singer Lance Bass, who was part of a celebrity duo competing on the show, prepared and served shrimp and grits for the show's judges. While the tape was rolling, another competitor, country singer Naomi Judd, made a comment about how, growing up, she didn't eat grits because her mother told her not to—she called them "poor people's food." Nearby, the singer Ray J, who was also appearing on the show, misinterpreted her comment and showed up on social media shortly after the event saying that Judd had called grits "slave food." A TMZ-fueled media backlash ensued, forcing the show's producers to reveal the raw footage and, consequently, Judd's actual comments about her feelings on grits.

Although Ray J misrepresented the exact words used, the

episode sparked the type of attention that continues to roil this country's ongoing dialogue about racism, this time through the vehicle of food. Ray J was not the first to reference grits as "slave food," and Naomi Judd is, unfortunately, one of many who consider grits, and likely many other traditionally Southern foods, something to be prepared and eaten only by the poor. Yes, comments like this throw a sticky web around the understanding of the dish— but it also helps to decipher how a dish like grits became a mainstream staple and even, in spite of the slur, offers an acknowledgment of those who should be given credit for carrying it there.

The story of grits cannot be told without including the fact that generations of enslaved Africans and, later, poor and repressed African Americans subsisted on a diet that included grits, a cheap nutritional fuel. (This is, of course, after thousands of years of indigenous people, bearing skin in other shades of red, brown, and yellow, carried the dish forward.) Generations of the enslaved were the primary processors, makers, cooks, and eaters of grits— but they also introduced and fed grits to generations of white Americans, too. During the time between settlers arriving on the shores of this country and the years just after the Civil War, people in every class were eating grits—and enslaved Africans were usually the ones preparing them.

So while the term *slave food* sits uncomfortably inside most white people's minds, mine included, it also reveals a more accurate and nuanced story, one that is often untold when it comes to understanding the dish's journey.

Around the same time of the Ray J–Judd dustup, a greater storm was brewing in the national food media sphere, specifically targeting the topic of appropriation. Across the country, including in Southern food media, articles were being written, and then dissected under a national microscope, about how and where certain dishes or traditions came from and who, if anyone, could claim ownership or hold the rights to tell the complete story. (My own research and writing of this book as a white, female author will likely face a similar fate.)

For grits, every major pivot point in the story line involves appropriation. It started with the fateful naming of the bowl of cracked maize. Later, as enslaved cooks prepared grits for their own people, as well as for the big-house masters, it went from being a Native American dish to being a "black" dish. Further along, as we moved into the twentieth century, grits became a grocery store staple, thanks to the white, male proprietors of companies like Quaker Oats and Aunt Jemima. Toward the 1990s, grits started showing up under shrimp tossed in gravy and were presented on upscale restaurant menus across the South, due to the reinterpretation of the dish called "breakfast shrimps," by a handful of affluent, white, male chefs.

So, after all that, is there any one culture, group, or person that owns this dish? And can there really be ownership when the origin story is so complex? More important than identifying any single owner, I've come to realize, is the acknowledgment of all who have carried the dish forward, and especially those who were carrying it directly prior to each turning point in the dish's history.

Native Roots

Doctor William Thomas—or Doc Bill, as he's known—an African American pathologist based outside of Atlanta, met Eastern

Cherokee natives Nancy and Tony Plemmons while working in a health clinic near their home in the North Georgia mountains. It took Doc Bill several months to get the couple, and specifically Nancy, a full-blood Cherokee, to speak with him, an outsider, and eventually to trust him. But after a few years of getting to know one another, the trio talked about creating a book of Cherokee recipes together. *Cherokee Cooking: From the Mountains and Gardens to the Table*, a book of recipes and stories, is the result of their collaboration, and brings forth a truly Cherokee voice and experience. As the book's editor, Doc Bill successfully assisted the Plemmonses in putting down their words, foods, and dishes.

Doc Bill and I met over dinner in Atlanta one night. He pulled out an iPad to show me photos of Nancy, as well as Tony, who had passed away years before. The photos revealed Nancy's process of nixtamalizing corn to make hominy. She worked outdoors, over a live fire, using an oversize cauldron and a paddle, a technique that had been practiced in that same exact way by Nancy's female ancestors for generations, Doc Bill explained.

As we talked, it became clear how close Doc Bill held his relationship with Nancy and Tony, and how much respect he had for the pair and their culture. It took years to produce the book, he explained. But from the very outset, he wanted it to be theirs—the words, recipes, stories, and structure. Doc Bill provided light editing and added a few notes throughout the text. Even the copyright belonged outright to the Plemmonses. And the Plemmonses relied on their tribe to make the book a community effort. There were stories from a Cherokee leader named Walker Calhoun, as well as other members of the tribe, named Lena and Albert, both fluent in Cherokee. "So it was written in such a fashion that if you cook [from it], you can learn a lot about Cherokee culture," Doc Bill said. "And even today, I think it's the best book on Cherokee culture that's out there."

Another book with a somewhat unobscured view of the role of grits, or corn dishes, in Native American life is *Buffalo Bird Woman's Garden*, originally published in 1917 by an anthropologist named Gilbert Wilson, who had embedded himself with the Hidatsa tribe in North Dakota. Written from the perspective of Maxidiwiac, a Hidatsa Sioux medicine woman, who was born in 1839, the book gives an oral history of the woman's gardening and farming rituals, much of which she picked up as a young girl. In the book, she recalls a story about how her tribe first started growing corn hundreds of years earlier. A rival tribe had attached parched ears of corn to arrows and shot them across the river into her tribe's territory, yelling the word, "Eat." Her tribe did eat the corn and later, encountering the other tribe, were gifted with half an ear of corn, which they pulled the kernels from and used to start planting their own corn.

Corn was a major part of their diet, she wrote. Occasionally, they would prepare it by starting with twelve handfuls of corn, which would go into a "corn mortar" shortly after breakfast; they would pound it a few handfuls at a time, causing the women to break a sweat. Those twelve handfuls would then get boiled in hot water for about thirty minutes, during which time the cook would skim the scum that rose to the top, tasting it to get a sense of how sticky it was becoming. (The skimmed liquid might also be fed to an infant who wasn't able to nurse.) Once the scum was very sticky, she said, they would add beans to the corn porridge and cook it all down into mush.

In both the Plemmonses' cookbook and the oration of Buffalo Bird Woman, the stories and recipes had been gathered and delivered by a nonindigenous person. Yes, they'd been collected with permission and in the first-person voices of the keepers of the knowledge. But the outsiders had been the vehicles—which made me consider that perhaps it wasn't so much that the information was lost as that it was being withheld—likely because so much had already been taken from these people with nothing given in return. Why share such a cultural treasure when it's just going to be appropriated, bastardized, and destroyed?

Despite the depth these two works offer on the Native American experience, they seem to exist in a bubble. The two texts are hardly, if ever, referenced in modern cookbooks, and have long been overlooked by the greater food community. Hopefully, in time, more stories like these will reveal a true point of origin for the dish—and help offer acknowledgment to those who brought these traditions to the present.

Bringing Awareness

There are now a handful of restaurant kitchens around the US preparing foods that are inspired by, or take cues from indigenous techniques, ingredients, and ritual. At the Mitsitam Café inside the National Museum of the American Indian, in Washington, DC, chef Freddie Bitsoie, who grew up on a Navajo reservation in Gallup, New Mexico, considers the restaurant itself to be an exhibition for native food. On the menu, which is organized by regions from throughout the Western hemisphere, he doesn't drill down to completely re-create indigenous dishes but rather takes inspiration from a few specific cultural affiliations and uses native ingredients in an effort to introduce guests to things they haven't tried before. During certain seasons there is a hominy posole on the menu as well as a hominy salad.

Freddie is an anthropologist as well as a chef. For years, he traveled the country, giving lectures on the topic of what it means to be Native American, and what goes into the concept of Native American cuisine. In the kitchen, he's bringing his own words to life, exploring native ingredients and cooking techniques, some traditional, some contemporary, in order to provide more context for certain regional flavors and cuisines.

In Minneapolis, Sean Sherman's forthcoming restaurant, as well as a concept called Water Works he is planning, will eventually lead to a food hub, which will support other regional tribes as they work to create other indigenous food businesses.

Both efforts, along with others across the continent, stand out for being vehicles through which more research and storytelling can be brought to light. And these two are notable in that they are primarily supported by people from within the native communities.

Still others are bringing awareness in their own way. For his own part, Anson Mills founder Glenn Roberts, who is white, knows all too well that having an awareness and respect for the people who did the work before him is essential to moving forward. Over the years, his own research and understanding of corn and rice in the Native American context has changed and been reframed dozens of times. "Two years ago, I would have told you that we were on the cusp, that we'd finally grasped the Southern food canon," he told me during my visit to Anson. "Now I realize we've lost more than a third of all Southern food for good, and most of that is undocumented." And, more than that, most of it is lost because those whose stories should have been loudest never even had a voice.

Glenn's mission and purpose, though, is only compelled by this notion. He harbors a great love for the earth and the foods from our past and present that have come from it—which is precisely why he is driven to better understand, and help others understand, Native American culture.

During my visit, he mentioned Nephi Craig, a member of the White Mountain Apache and Navajo tribe who, after attending culinary school, founded NACA, or Native American Culinary Association. Nephi is a chef at the Sunrise Park Resort's Summit Restaurant in Whiteriver, Arizona. The resort is owned by the White Mountain Apache tribe, and all of Nephi's kitchen employees are members of the tribe as well. What Nephi does, Glenn explained, goes into "pantheistic elements of cookery, where you go forage and you gather stones and energy pieces to go with that food and you use that stuff to cook the food, then you have to take it back and return it, after you eat the foraged stuff."

Glenn was also mindful to talk about teosinte and the work of Martha Willcox, a geneticist at the International Maize and Wheat Improvement Center in Mexico (CIMMYT). She's the number-one point person for anything maize-related in this hemisphere, he intoned.

Martha's name had been circulating in culinary circles for her work with landrace improvement in Mexico. Recently, she'd been cited for helping a company called Masienda identify heirloom varieties of corn and connect with members of Oaxaca's farming community in order to bring heirloom corn into chefs' hands in the United States, for the purpose of making tortillas. Of the fifty-nine landrace varieties of that country's corn—corn that is locally adapted to Oaxaca—Masienda had brought as many as fifteen into American kitchens, including varieties like white and blue bolita and white olotillo corn. In the process, Masienda was paying a fair wage to farmers in Mexico, most of whom live below the poverty line. Martha's work, and the work of the CIM-MYT, was in both preserving maize diversity as well as Mexico's culinary traditions.

I asked if Glenn had ever considered crossing teosinte to create a form of maize, almost like a historical experiment, which, considering his work with plant life and varieties, seemed like something he might try.

He paused before answering. "You know, I don't believe in all that stuff because it's a nice easy answer," he said, referring to the theory that thousands of years ago, it was human hands working with teosinte to create maize.

What he meant was this: Maize is a thorny topic for any indigenous culture, and gets even more challenging when you take it out of a native context. There is a spiritual and cultural aspect of maize that doesn't often get talked about, especially in culinary circles in the US. More than having a connection to a traditional system of worship, the full story of maize goes back to creationism. In Mesoamerican legends, maize itself is an active element in the creation story, with humans literally emerging from a cob of white corn. Maize, for some Native Americans, exists in a context of spirituality, meaning they see far more than variety or carbon layering or cross-pollination. They see their own lineage, their people, their creator. Corn as god and humanity combined.

This raises extremely emotional issues for indigenous people. And for Glenn, who operates as a modern-day seeds person, it's a motivator to continue developing awareness and respect for the cultural touchstone. If he didn't have that awareness—or if he'd attempted to go into these tribes, procure corn seed, take it out, and monetize it—he would have been shut out decades ago.

(I recalled my conversation with Doc Bill about working with the Plemmonses. "There were certain things, religious and spiritual, that they wouldn't let me know about. And really, I couldn't know about them. If you weren't Cherokee, you couldn't get in," he'd told me.)

And yet Glenn does attempt to offer context. "Have you heard of walk ins?" he asked me on the day of my visit. "So, the entire process of maize cookery involves movement, it involves nine levels of pantheism, and movement. It's done without animals, because pre-Columbian, you did not have conveyance, right? Humans were the conveyance. Walking is part of the experience of bringing hot points of energy into maize cookery," he explained.

I took it all to mean that those who are still growing and cooking maize using native methods were doing so on a level that most commercial farmers today would deem nuts. But not Glenn. And not the tribes he's learned all this from. To them, that process is life-giving.

And so, he went on, any work he does in seed saving, any requests he receives for native-produced ingredients, and basically anything he "takes" from Native American tribes is never sold, but always paid for. "We don't monetize any of that stuff, ever," he said. "And we pay back to the tribes, for all [that] we're doing with their stuff," he added.

When unleashed, Glenn's memory bank also offers a casual and fractured view of the various associations he's had with Native Americans over the years. There was the Jesuit mission in San Diego, where he spent time as a kid, when his parents, who were both singers, were rehearsing. There were natives at the mission, mostly young girls, cooking in the space out back on their comals, or griddles, using masa to make corn cakes—that community had been in place four hundred years before Glenn arrived, he claimed. And, being a self-proclaimed "chowhound" as a kid, he would hang around the women while they were making food. There was also his grandfather's grandfather who lived out on the Ohio frontier, where the only doctors were Native Americans. "My native attention ran deep," he said.

And then, he casually dropped in a story of Carlos Castaneda, an anthropologist and mystic who wrote about natives and shamans in northern Mexico, who he "hung out with for a while in Mexico." Next, he was on to a tale of Papi, a chef who had worked with William Randolph Hearst before retiring to Idaho to live with the Kutenai tribe. Glenn, hearing about Papi's settlement, went off to Idaho in search of the chef. "The first time I met him, he was crawling down a corn row with his wife. She was singing, he was patting the ground, and I thought they were totally nuts." He snorted, then paused for a split second before adding, "That's where I got my first ideas of working for the tribes for free."

Later, he explained his theory on the five transformative processes for making grits: alcohol ferment, acidic ferment, acido basilisk, parch, nixtamalization. "If you can combine all five processes, you'd first sprout the grain, then you'd do both ferments, alcohol and acidic, to make the equivalent of alcoholic vinegar, then parch it, then you nixtamalize it. When you combine all five transformation processes, this is your perfect food," he said. I took that to mean that, in a Native context, applying all these processes would allow the corn to nourish the body properly.

"I'm not supposed to talk about this, though," he added, smiling as though revealing a secret. And he probably was—these were not his techniques to share. He'd been exposed to these ancient, native processes but that didn't mean he'd been given permission to pass them on. And yet they practically spilled out of him, as though these thoughts, which had been swirling intensely in his mind for many years, couldn't stay put. I saw within Glenn the struggle that many in his position face. As a white person of means, with privilege, he is intentionally making an effort to lift up and celebrate the foods that have been appropriated from another culture. And yet, however sincere his actions, his own status and background further perpetuate the perception of appropriation.

What Glenn does try to do is offer an introduction to the original seed carriers, to the unwritten, often untold history that leads up to this point in maize culture. By introducing the concept that there are still those who might look at a dish like grits through the lens of faith, spirituality, and creationism, he at least provides a stepping stone to better understanding.

Black Roots

There's a short, squat Piggly Wiggly supermarket that sits tucked away near the town center of St. George, South Carolina. It's a Piggly Wiggly like any other: the white outline of a chubby-cheeked, paper-hat-wearing pig marks the exterior, which is otherwise all brick and siding. It's small, though, more like the size of today's standard gas station than a grocery store.

The size perfectly complements the town itself. St. George is small, and sleepy, and slow. People there like it that way. An hour northwest of Charleston, it's tucked squarely inland, away from the marsh-lined coast but still peppered with palmetto trees and set with sandy soil. About two thousand people call it home today.

Though boarded-up windows mark many of the low brick storefronts that cluster together to just barely make up a downtown, one can imagine a once bustling community center, where townspeople used to shop within a few blocks for everything from shoes to books to groceries. Today, those buildings tell a different story, one similar to so many small Southern towns, where just a handful of the original, family-owned businesses hang on while new banks with fine landscaping are dropped in.

The face of St. George's business district started to change when big-box stores like Walmart arrived. (One of the closest, in nearby Walterboro, opened in 1989.) Still, you can occasionally find shoppers popping into the Weeks' Department Store, which hangs on tight to its spot in the center of town; or community members gathering together to fill the seats of the 1920s-era Lourie Theatre, when the town's annual theatrical production is listed on the marquee. Traces of the old St. George spirit can also still be found, naturally, at the Piggly Wiggly.

In 1985, the manager of the local Piggly Wiggly, Bill Hunter, had a visit from one of his many grocery brokers; this one was from the Quaker Oats Company. During what was probably a weekly ritual, Bill and the broker caught up for a bit, exchanging news and swapping stories, before Bill placed his order. That's when the broker brought up something that had been on his mind.

"We sure ship a lot of grits to this little town," the broker commented. Bill nodded in agreement—yes, St. George loved its grits. He let the thought go until a short while later, when another broker, this one for Jim Dandy products, made a similar comment—St. George really ordered a lot of grits, the man said. In those days, Jim Dandy was owned by Martha White Foods Inc., which had paid $5 million in 1981 for the business, then the second-largest producer of grits, in an effort to take on Quaker in the grits category. (Quaker, Aunt Jemima, and Jim Dandy have long been the top three sellers of grits in the country, with a combined total of nearly 5 million Americans claiming to eat ten or more portions of their grits each week.)

Bill, curious about the common observation, took it to the store's owners, John Walters and George Axson. The three put their heads around this notion—that St. George, South Carolina, was serious about grits—and after a little more research, discovered that, yes indeed, both cereal companies shipped more grits to this part of South Carolina than anywhere else in the world. St. George, they concluded, ate the most grits per capita anywhere. To celebrate this revelation, the town held its first World Grits Festival the following spring, with the local store, as well as Quaker and Jim Dandy, acting as major sponsors. The festival still takes place in the town each April.

My first visit to the World Grits Festival was also my first visit to St. George. Though my grits research would take me all over the South, I noticed that no area seemed to serve up and celebrate grits with as much enthusiasm and genuine pride as St. George seemed to do. At the festival, I asked a few of the residents if they had any theories on why people in that area loved their grits so much.

"Well, we just have always loved our grits," one lady hummed to me.

An older gentleman, as he served me a plate of grits and catfish, surmised, "It's because they're so good with gravy."

But it was a longer answer that stood out. It came from a life-long St. Georgian, Steve Franks, a volunteer organizer of the festival who held a day job as a gun salesman at Walmart. Steve thought the tradition went way back, and was mostly due to the old "camp meeting site."

"Back in the old times, say, in the 1800s, there were circuit preachers that didn't have churches. These circuit preachers would travel and come to these campgrounds where everybody who lived in a certain area would get together to go to church. They might stay a week or two. We still have the biggest camp meeting site just out here in St. George, called Indian Fields," he explained. "It's a big social thing around here. People still go and they make the biggest meals you can imagine—and grits are served at all the meals. Now, some tents might have a hundred people show up to eat, and grits are always served. There's a tremendous amount of grits at these things."

I'd never heard of camp meetings, I explained. "Well," he said, "you ought to go see one of the sites for yourself. It's just up the road a bit. It's one of the largest still in use." Then he gave me directions to Indian Fields.

A mile or so away from the central district's cluster of buildings, the scenery opened up to reveal sandy fields, a couple of small churches, and a John Deere supply store. I turned left at a sign that read "Indian Fields" and headed straight toward a tall patch of pine trees. As I got closer to the cluster of trees, the road turned slightly, guiding me past a long, pastured field on the left. The road narrowed into the width of a driveway at the edge of the trees, and just beyond, I spotted a few buildings sitting shoulder to shoulder. I continued pulling forward and realized that I was looking at the back side of a large circle of two-story wooden cabins.

Slowly, I bumped along the road, trying to see between the cabins. The air was still except for chirping birds and an occasional gust of wind, which set off the gunshot-like *smack* of metal roofing tiles banging against one another.

The cabins all faced inward toward one another in a mile-wide ring. At the center, a sprawling lawn was peppered with spindly pine trees that surrounded a massive, open-air tabernacle set with benches.

Each cabin, most creaking and barren, had its own open-air kitchen set toward the back of the ground floor. Some had wide brick hearths, others had cast-iron stoves. Chimney pipes climbed up out of each roof and I could see that most of them had sinks with running water as well as overhead lights. The dirt floors were scattered with some hay, but mostly the ground was bare. Out front, facing the lawn, front porches appeared primed for gathering and socializing. The tabernacle at the center, rustically constructed from large beams of wood, was the size of a church—large enough to hold nearly a thousand people.

Indian Fields, founded in 1801, was one of the first camp meeting sites to exist in the southeast. Large religious gatherings started taking place all over the area in the late 1700s as part of the Great Awakening of the region. They occurred around the arrival of circuit-riding preachers, like Bishop Francis Asbury, a founder of American Methodism, who rode from town to town across America, stopping for several days at a time to preach to a community and staying in people's homes.

In the southeast, these meetings, which typically happened at the end of the harvest season, soon swelled to a point where the only location large enough to hold the throngs of people was an open field. Wagons and tents were set up and gathered into a circle so that families could camp and worship together.

Indian Fields is one of only five South Carolina camp meeting sites that remain in use. Set about three miles from the center of St. George, it's named for the Indian Field United Methodist Church, founded in 1787. Bishop Asbury wrote in his journal about preaching at Indian Fields in 1801 and 1803. The circle of cabins I stood among contained updated versions of structures that had been erected in 1848—there were ninety-nine in all.

Over the years, the buildings had suffered fires, floods, and disrepair—but they were always rebuilt, the circle forever intact, the shape and footprint remaining in place for more than two hundred years. Each "tent," as they were called, was passed down, usually within the same family, from generation to generation.

While Indian Fields is a camp meeting site that specifically serves a white population, a few miles away in Harvleyville sits St. Paul Camp Ground, an African American site that was established in 1875. The tradition of African Americans gathering for worship in a similar setting had started around the same time as the Great Awakening—but because those gatherings were populated by the enslaved, the meetings were held in secret, hidden spaces, with worshippers gathering beneath a natural brush arbor deep in the woods.

Each fall, communities still gather, separately, at these camps—generations of families converging on the sites, taking time off work to convene for a week. The sermons heard these days are not the same fiery preachings of hell and brimstone that might have rattled hearts and minds a hundred years ago. Instead, it's a softer message, similar to one that's spoken on any given Sunday at Methodist churches throughout the South. During the week-long event, there are usually prayer calls three times throughout the day. And while the community that convenes there comes primarily to worship, the long-standing tradition is, to the minds of many, more than a religious experience. It's a way for them to preserve the old times, to stick close to family, and to find communion with those they've come to know year after year.

Though the division between Indian Fields and St. Paul is racial, there are ties that bind both camps—mostly, the food that's served at both sites, and the people preparing the meals. Between the prayers and family gatherings, there is, and always has been, plenty of food. Steve Franks, who told me where to find Indian Fields, talked lovingly about the meals. Having been a regular attendee himself for years, he explained that many families hired cooks to come with them to the campsite each year, loading up enough food for the week. (Grits, he noted repeatedly, were often part of the menu, served at breakfast, lunch, and dinner in some kitchens.) But at Indian Fields, several of the people cooking, even now, are black. They are paid well to cook for the families they serve. And when, a week or so later, the same type of gathering occurs at St. Paul Camp Ground for a strictly black community, those same cooks are sometimes cooking at or attending those services, too.

Though the African Americans hired to cook at Indian Fields today are paid, originally they were not. Many of the cooks who prepared the meals at Indian Fields prior to the Civil War were enslaved African Americans, who used the rudimentary kitchens and outdoor stoves or hearths to prepare breakfast, lunch, and dinner for entire families every day for a week or more. Even then, grits were on the table for everyone—black and white.

Stepping inside one of the more rustic cabins, I saw that a single lightbulb hung from the kitchen ceiling, and the stove, a sheet of steel over a coal box, was built into a crumbling brick hearth. I imagined a time before electricity and considered how a cook working in a space like this might make grits. This basic square room, with its hearth, single table set to one side, bucket and faucet that acted as a sink, and a few old hooks on the wall to hold tools, was not much different, except perhaps larger, than a typical slave kitchen. If hominy was produced in a space like this, the labor would have occupied the better part of a day, as the corn had to be cooked with wood ash for several hours before the hulls could be slipped off. Then, if it was to be dried, the cook needed to find the space to set the corn to dry. If they were making something more simple, like a pot of dry-ground corn—in some cases, ground laboriously by hand after a dawn-to-dusk workday—mixed with water, the pot would have taken up a large part of the hearth space.

As I ran my hand over the surfaces and pulled the door of the coal box opened, I felt a sense of the effort it would take to prepare just one single meal in that space. But just because I could imagine it didn't mean I could ever fully understand what life was like for the enslaved.

I felt the weight of my own whiteness standing in that cooking space. There was so much I didn't know, couldn't know, about the realities of an enslaved life. I felt my own ignorance spread through me, a mix of guilt and confusion over my inability to fully comprehend all the complicated stories a place like this held.

What I needed was a voice—a living, breathing voice—to help me get closer to the story.

The first I turned to was food historian and author Michael Twitty, a black Jew who is based in Virginia, and traces his roots deep into the tumultuous reaches of the enslaved South. He's become a student of black food history, as well as a prolific writer and speaker, challenging many preconceived notions of what the South was and is—most notably by shedding light on many voices that have not yet been heard or properly attributed. In his book *The Cooking Gene* he explores the foods his ancestors ate and prepared and uses those foods as a way to address today's current understanding and definition of Southern food.

I called Michael with many questions, but mostly I wanted to know how slaves cooked and ate grits. How often did they eat them? And what did it feel like, smell like, and taste like to eat them in that context? Michael was thoughtful, as though he was used to white people asking complicated questions about his race disguised as simple questions about food. He answered them through his personal lens, one he'd crafted with thorough research, as well as knowledge he'd gained directly from his own ancestors.

His intentional and proverbial "we" addressed the enslaved and their ancestors.

"We were used to eating food that engaged us physically," he explained. "We were used to standing at the mortar and pestle, the music that was produced, beating hominy. The music and the physicality of it—and this is not being romantic—that was a part of your culture, your way of life, your spirituality."

Meanwhile, he pointed out, the enslaved were, in many cases, also cooking in the big house, probably preparing a similar meal for the people who were enslaving them. Grits, he affirmed, were the food of everyone in the South, thanks, especially, to the black hands making the food.

"A lot of these white Southern planters grew up with women raising them who were black. I mean, from a practical standpoint, what are you going to do, make a separate breakfast for your kids and for his kids? No. They're going to have the same pot, and they all eat from the same pot. It was something that people shared, like it or not," he said.

Standing in the camp meeting site, I could see Michael's theory playing out, both back when slavery existed legally in this region, and even today, as the weight of that historical reality is still being grappled with.

As writer and soul food expert Adrian Miller writes in his book *Soul Food*, "Prestige foods and stigmatized foods alike crossed racial and class lines in each direction."[10] He goes on to describe cornshuckings, which occurred across the South on large plantations, usually in the late fall once the corn was harvested. Slaves on these plantations considered it an important agricultural event because its success "was critical to having enough grain supplies to last an entire year." Meanwhile, yeoman farmers "who didn't have enough slaves to do the massive amount of work required for corn grinding . . . often had to complete cornshucking and corn-grinding tasks themselves."[11]

Both writers point out that these cooking rituals, though grueling and labor-intensive, became part of the food traditions of the enslaved and were later passed along even after slavery was abolished. Cornshucking and grinding, and preparing corn as grits or hominy, were acts that brought a community together, even under the circumstances. And the dishes themselves, which were regularly eaten in poor living conditions or under challenging circumstances, gave comfort in the form of nourishment to the enslaved. That comfort is what still gathers communities today.

The celebratory camp meetings are, to this day, racially divided. Camp meetings preserve an essential element of each micro-community's culture: the fellowship, the traditions, the families, and the food. Black and white, the people in these communities share the same ideals, and each group is uplifted and spiritually fulfilled by these annual events. The idea that these groups remain divided may seem complicated on the surface— as complicated as the region itself—until you hear people within each group talk about why.

Documentary filmmaker Stan Woodward spent several weeks at the camp meeting sites of South Carolina back in the early 2000s. His films, which are available through a service called Folkstreams, offer a rare and important glimpse of the people who still attend these annual meetings. As a first-timer, Stan was met with open arms by those who wished to share their stories of these places. He visited several of the sites, including Indian Fields, St. Paul, Cypress, and Cattle Creek, during their meeting times.

With his camera turned on, he gently questioned attendees about their reasons for coming year after year, and for their thoughts on why these meetings still took place. One question he kept coming back to was: Why are these groups still separate?

Members at St. Paul and Indian Fields used different words to say the same thing, but the message came through clear and simple: we want to preserve *our* way of doing things.

Their interest in preserving one camp's specific culture or traditions offers conflicting outcomes. On the one hand, these communities are tightly bound units that will likely remain that way thanks to the efforts of so many generations. On the other, in a region like the South where racial tensions still divide people, these separate meetings could be keeping people from getting beyond their differences and closer to their commonalities, such as their love for certain foods, especially grits.

Through the lens of Stan's footage, it's clear that food is at the heart of all camp meetings. Whether it's the days-long preparation of hash and barbecue or a simple pot of grits stirred throughout the morning, food prepared at camp meetings helps anchor each of these communities. Grits are certainly not the only dish these groups have in common, but the corn-based porridge does stand apart for its equalizing capabilities. Perceived as slave food, poor people's food, fuel, sustenance, breakfast, *and* comfort to so many, the humble dish, though shared in spirit and not reality, still manages to give anyone eating it equal footing.

Blended Roots

Like much of the South, the Lowcountry is a complicated place. Loosely shaped like an oblong triangle, the region encompasses a stretch of land along the South Carolina and Georgia coastlines. And for the past several hundred years, human relationships in the region have been fraught. From those halcyon pre-settlement days when indigenous people fished and hunted along those shores, to the occupation and annihilation of those people by various conquerors; from the rise of plantation life and the labor-intensive agricultural work of all of those who were enslaved, to the dismantling of the slavery system and destruction of those properties during the Civil War; from the protection and isolation the Sea Islands provided the former slaves, which gave rise to a stronger identity for the Gullah Geechee people, to the eventual overdevelopment and highway- and bridge-building era that brought us to where we are today: The Lowcountry is one very narrow stage on which many of America's more horrific historical story lines have played out, and today, it reveals threads of those themes on a daily basis to anyone who calls it home.

This does not make it much different from other parts of the South. But it is unique in that it remains a rich stew of cultures, simmering with those story lines, as well as the various people who have populated it. It's a place where physical structures, like buildings, homes, and statues, stand as historical reminders of the past—but are abutted with the markers of shiny new developments that slowly threaten to erase that same past.

In a region where that's happening, names, identifying symbols, and cultural terms can come loaded. Whether it's a glossy magazine called *Garden & Gun* debuting a few days before a mass shooting at Virginia Tech, or the Charleston Wine + Food Festival hosting a sold-out Gullah luncheon to a mostly white audience, the visuals and messaging around certain cultural themes can get complicated.

This occurred to me the first time I tried those Jimmy Red grits at Husk Nashville. When they arrived at the table, the server announced that the grits were produced by Geechie Boy, a mill on South Carolina's Edisto Island.

First, there was the spelling, "geechie," which was different than the traditional Geechee written in reference to the Gullah Geechee cultural community. But there was also the fact that the name belonged to a market and milling business that was owned by a young white couple.

I eventually made my way to Edisto to meet the team at Geechie Boy. Passing through the piney landscape and under canopies of live oaks draped in Spanish moss, I reached the long arc of the Edisto Island Bridge. Compared to the overdevelopment of much of the region, this Sea Island felt nearly untouched—one end was a quaint, quiet beach destination, but most of the island, formerly marked by plantations, was undeveloped.

Just over the Russell Creek Bridge, the Geechie Boy Market sat a short distance from the road on the right. The day I stopped by, co-owner Betsy Johnsman agreed to show me around. Along with her husband, Greg, she and various members of her family kept the growing and milling operations running.

When I arrived, she introduced herself in a kind voice matched by large, soft brown eyes. With her faint freckles, long brown hair, and big, toothy smile, she had the warm, open face of a grade school teacher. We walked over a length of field toward a squat wooden building with "Geechie Boy Market & Mill" painted in tall red letters across the side. A raised garden bed rimmed the exterior, and there was a comically large red Adirondack chair out front, beckoning visitors to stop for a snapshot. Betsy led me inside the building and over toward the mill.

"We started out as farmers," she explained, referring to herself and Greg—but she'd come from a long tradition of farming, too. Her father, Adair, started farming when he was fifteen years old, farther upstate in Sumter County. It was her mother, Boone, named after Boone Hall Plantation in Mount Pleasant, whose family had ties to the Edisto land. Generations of Betsy's family had owned or worked the land, most of which had long ago been segmented into plantations that had once produced everything from cotton to bumper cabbage crops.

"A few of the plantations we farm now were my family's," she said. By easily offering up the fact that her family had once owned plantations here, and likely slaves, she seemed to be saying that while it was a difficult truth, it was one she and her husband grappled with openly and regularly, especially considering the name of the market.

Betsy met Greg while attending Clemson, where she'd gotten a degree in animal veterinary science. Greg Johnsman was the college's last poultry major before they closed the program. Greg had been raised in Greenville, South Carolina, where, at an early age, he had been exposed to mountain culture. "He learned to mill from moonshiners," Betsy said. "That's what he would do on the weekends in college. You know, my friends and I, we'd go out on the boat, or we'd go camping and he'd be like, 'Oh, I went and milled.'"

The moonshiners he learned from were using a portable mill powered by a huge, old, hit-or-miss Stover Engine—an antique throwback from the early 1900s. Jack Brock, a third-generation mountain miller, taught Greg about the machine, giving Greg his first taste of gear-nerdery. During college, Greg took Betsy out to visit Mr. Brock a few times and to watch how they milled. "It was beautiful," she told me. "It made these big puffs of smoke—it was always a big production, and I just fell in love with it."

Betsy brought Greg back to Edisto after college and the two picked up the family mantle—but instead of going into commercial tomato production, like Betsy's father had done, they decided to grow heirloom varieties. They started by planting three acres, which, Betsy admitted, was a lot of heirloom tomatoes for two people to farm. And they had to have more than a few conversations with Adair to convince him that it was financially viable. Being used to the industry standard of a perfectly round tomato, he called their crop ugly.

"I said, 'We're getting about twenty-six dollars for that flat.' And he said, 'How is that possible?' Then he tasted one, and just went, 'Wow,'" she said.

With her father's help, Betsy and Greg's three-acre operation eventually grew into ten acres, but after a few years, they scaled it back. "There aren't enough people in Charleston to eat that many heirlooms," she explained. Through a packinghouse, they would ship the crop up to brokers in New York and Chicago, but the transportation was tough on the finicky heirlooms.

Even as their tomato operation blossomed, Greg was always looking to mill. Like an itch that needed scratching, his desire to operate and tinker with old machines nagged at him. He'd learned about an intact 1945 mill that a man named Lamar Berry was holding on to up in the Midstate, in Saluda, South Carolina. Mr. Berry, who'd discovered the mill and an old grits separator abandoned in a warehouse, had the forethought to store them both securely, keeping the machines intact—a rare decision, considering most mills and grits separators had gone out of style years before, when larger cereal-making companies had put to use industrial, steel roller milling techniques. Many of the older stone-grinding machines had either been melted or broken down for parts, or left to fall into disrepair—similar to the ones being located and restored by Brian Hege and the team at Meadows Mills. Greg asked his mentor, Jack Brock, for advice and Jack encouraged him to take the machine and get it running again. Lamar agreed to give it to Greg—but only on the condition that Greg put it to use for the community by displaying it in public in order to show people how it worked. Greg honored the requirement, and the mill now sits inside the market, a space that has become a popular gathering spot for the community each summer.

Greg and Betsy eventually replaced the engine and updated some of the exterior metal work and wood paneling, and also revived the working parts of the mill and separator. The separator was painted a dusty red and had "grits" and "high speed chicken feed" hand-painted across the front in black lettering. Standing before it, I got the sense of the machine's age—parts of it were new, but the black steel on the wheels and rusted, beat-up metal MEADOWS MILL placard revealed a lifetime of hard labor. This mill had been put to good use over the years. An antique elevator system was set between the two machines; tiny pockets attached to a conveyor belt moved up around a loop—the system captured the milled grains, pulling them upward, and deposited them into the separator. The Johnsmans ran the mill one or two days a week for the public to see, and to keep up with their production. "She makes this great noise, this *clickety clack*." Betsy beamed.

There were mills all over the property, many in pieces or with parts missing. Greg's passion was restoring them and putting them back into use, either for his own company's needs or to give back to others. Greg's most prized piece was from 1847, the first fully American-made mill, meaning all of its parts and pieces were made in the US—from the stones to the metal to the wood. It was built at a time when foundries had started to appear in the US; before the 1840s, most millstones and the metals to build out the mill bodies came from Europe. But this piece, which was produced in Cincinnati, Ohio, was made completely from American-made materials, many of which came from the South. Greg also had one of the earliest grits separators, which Meadows started producing in 1906, along with the original advertisement for the machine.

Betsy's pride was reserved for a different piece, though. They had in their possession Edisto Island's original grain separator. They'd recovered it from a friend of the family who had called saying he had an old seed cleaner to get rid of. He told them if they could come and retrieve it, it was theirs to keep. "We got it out and saw that it was actually a separator, and on the inside it read 'Edisto Island' and I was like, 'Holy cow, Greg, this is from the area,'" Betsy explained. They planned to restore it and set it up inside the market house, in order to give it back to the community it had been built to serve nearly a hundred years ago.

The discussion of community brought me back to the name of the business, Geechie Boy. I asked Betsy how they came to use it as their own. Her explanation was complicated—and also telling of some Southerners' abilities to paint the past with a soft shroud of light. The name came with the market itself, she explained. It was once owned by Raymond L. Tumbleston, then a seventysomething islander who Betsy's father had partnered with long ago. As a child, Mr. Tumbleston, as Betsy called him, was nicknamed "the Geechie boy" on account of his thick accent. Mr. Tumbleston was a white man, but had developed the dialect based on how and where he was raised.

Being surrounded by the mostly African American Gullah Geechee community, many white people are also linked to the culture. Mr. Tumbleston, as well as Betsy's mom, Boone, spoke in the same lilting, abbreviated, Creole-style of English—Geechee. So the fact that in the 1940s, Mr. Tumbleston, who would have been five or six years old, had garnered a nickname based on his accent wasn't surprising. But the name stuck, and he used it as the name of the farm and vegetable market he opened when he was grown.

"I thought we might change the name," Betsy admitted. Both she and Greg questioned the perception of it. Her concerns even led her to do some research, she said. What she found was a version of that region's history that isn't widely written.

The Gullah Geechee culture was centered around the descendants of enslaved West Africans and Central Africans who once labored on the area's many rice plantations. After the Civil War, many plantation slaves, now freed, stayed where they had been enslaved, taking advantage of the isolation that the accessible-by-boat-only Sea Islands allowed. For generations, these freed black men and women lived on the islands, maintaining their cultural practices and heritage without much interference or disruption. In this way, they were able to preserve their traditions, language, and foodways.

But, as Betsy described it, there is a more layered side of this story to be told. The way she read it, a number of other people from varying heritages, including Native Americans, French, Spanish, and Italians—some former plantation owners—were woven into the fabric of these same communities after the Civil War. The freed slaves and their descendants had stayed on islands like Edisto—but so, too, had white people of differing ethnicities and backgrounds, some of whom returned after the war to find a completely altered, and ravaged, landscape. Still, she learned, these communities coexisted and likely comingled, some existing in poverty or on only what the land could provide, in a way that put a child Mr. Tumbleston's age in close proximity to many other Gullah Geechee families.

By keeping the name of the market intact, she said, Betsy and Greg felt they were honoring Mr. Tumbleston—and to them, that had more value than the complicated story lines the name evoked, or the perception that those not familiar with the layered story Betsy offered might take away. In the end, she said, "The community wouldn't allow us to change it. That included African

Americans, and members of the Gullah Geechee community, all of whom expressed the sentiment that the name represented the community, not just their operation. In the couple's mind, the question had been addressed and answered in a way that gave them permission to keep the name in place.

Regardless of the reaction the couple has received about the name, Greg and Betsy stand by their decision to keep it. By reviving heritage grains on Edisto under the name Geechie Boy, they believe they represent the best of their community, and respectfully maintain a place and piece of history that many people, black and white, have a stake in, all while sustaining a small family farming operation.

In Full Color

Through learning about Glenn Roberts and how Anson Mills has made an impact on the greater milling industry, I dug deeper into the world of grain milling around Columbia, South Carolina. That "secret capital of the grits world" has provided a platform for large players like Anson and Adluh, as well as some small local upstarts, including the Congaree Milling Company. Its owner, Ken DuBard, and original miller, Lawrence Burwell, left Anson around 2012 to form a two-man operation that ran out of a restaurant kitchen in Columbia. They'd created their niche by milling hybrid organic corns—and also producing true hominy grits using nixtamalization. Though nixtamalizing corn to produce hominy was something Glenn and his team at Anson would occasionally do for chefs, hominy wasn't a product they sold frequently. For Ken, it became just the thing to help his business stand apart.

I met Ken and Lawrence at their millsite, a pizza and beer restaurant called Dano's that sits near the leafy residential outskirts of downtown Columbia. Working out of a restaurant kitchen was what had allowed them to experiment with nixtamalization in the first place—they had a commercial-grade preparation space, and once the corn had been soaked with calcium hydroxide (pickling lime), they used the restaurant's pizza ovens to dry the corn kernels before passing them through their 8-inch stone burr Meadows mill. They also roasted some of their corns using the pizza ovens and milled those into grits or polenta, producing a deep, toasty flavor once the product was cooked. Working with yellow, white, and blue organic corns sourced from the Midwest, Congaree's products ranged from corn flours and meals to quick grits and even stone-cut toasted oats. The pair operated the mill from four a.m. until nine or ten, when the restaurant staff started to arrive, and might mill as many as five or six hundred pounds of product per week.

I smiled when I grasped the lean, muscular outstretched hand of Lawrence Burwell, a tall and lanky black man. So many of the millers and grits producers I'd come across, I explained, were white men. Lawrence, as Congaree's head miller, was one of just a few African American millers I tracked down while researching grits. And, compared to almost everyone else I came across, he and Ken were young—under the age of forty-five.

Growing up, Lawrence was a military kid—he was raised on bases, he explained. Germany, Fort Benning. He tried college, but "got into some trouble," he said, with a sheepish grin. "I landed back here in Columbia with my dad when I was nineteen. I went back to school . . . eventually," he added.

Ken, meanwhile, was a lifelong South Carolinian who could trace his lineage back generations. He grew up on his family's land in Cedar Creek, northeast of Columbia. "My family's been here since the beginning of time," he told me—implying pre–Civil War. "There are some buildings out there on the property that are colonial," he added.

He occasionally goes back to visit, he said. "But I'm not one for all that 'lost cause' stuff—it's still a thing around there." He shrugged, glancing over at Lawrence.

Lawrence gave him a sidelong glance, then chuckled. "Man, I sure hope not," he said, shoving an elbow into Ken's ribs.

Agriculture had been a focus for Ken's family—one of his grandfathers had been a cotton farmer in the 1940s but gave up after a few bouts with boll weevils. Ken's father didn't farm but they did have a large family garden. One of Ken's brothers, who went into agriculture, was now a farmer in the area—he grows corn, Ken said, but not enough for what he and Lawrence were trying to accomplish. Instead, they were finding better luck, and consistency, sourcing organic corn from the Midwest.

"Plus," Ken added carefully, "most of the farms I could get it from, Glenn's already gone to, so I'm a bit shy about approaching them."

Did he feel he was competing with Anson? I asked.

"If it wasn't for Glenn paving this path, we wouldn't have been able to find a market, to come in and do what we're doing," Ken said, weighing his words carefully. "And they're doing thousands of pounds when we're doing hundreds. We also focus a lot on accounts here in Columbia, whereas Glenn has accounts all over the world. So, no . . . " he added. But I could tell he didn't want to say anything on the record that would piss off his former boss— he wasn't about to offer any indication as to why the two parted ways, either.

"He taught us a lot," Lawrence interjected. "About milling, about production. But we have a chance now to do it our way, and to do something new," he said. "Plus, who doesn't love making their own hours?"

Together, the guys had built a thriving small business, with Lawrence milling and Ken running the culinary aspects of the operation—nixtamalizing, roasting—as well as the marketing, business, and sales end of things. They were selling at a few weekly farmers' markets in the area, including the largest, Soda City, where vendors took up three blocks every Saturday morning throughout the year. They also sold and hand-delivered to local restaurants, with their accounts ranging from a nearby quick-service breakfast and lunch joint, the Gourmet Shop, to the Oak Table, a high-end steak house and bar.

I asked if I could come by the restaurant to see their milling operation in process the next morning. Though I wasn't sure I'd make it by the four a.m. start time, I did manage to get there, armed with high-test coffee, by about five thirty. I stepped in from the pitch-black morning to find the kitchen at Dano's brightly lit and humming noisily. Ken stood by a stainless-steel table, checking his phone, with two cups of coffee in front of him. He looked haggard.

We walked toward Lawrence, who was kneeling down and fiddling with the mill, which they'd rolled out toward the middle of an open space on the tiled kitchen floor. Ken pulled open a white plastic bag to show me a pile of blue corn kernels that he had already nixtamalized, then handed me a fork. I reached in and poked at a few kernels, pulling out the softened corn.

"Taste that?" he said, taking his own bite. "I think it tastes a little like bubble gum. And I also get some strawberry," he said. I tasted popcorn and some underlying fruitiness. The flavor was big and bright. Ken opened another bag that was full of roasted yellow kernels—those would be milled into polenta, he explained. They smelled like burnt toast in a way that made my mouth water.

It was going to be a slow day for them. A big storm was coming through, which meant they were likely going to have to shut down the Saturday market due to rain. Ken delivered the news with a small tinge of positivity. This was day five of a week of early mornings—a day off from the market for their two-man operation might mean a hit in sales, but could also deliver a much-needed respite. Lawrence had been out late the night before, he admitted, and Ken, though he was acting chipper, looked exhausted. I could tell his mind was elsewhere as he looked over the order sheet to see what was left to mill for the week.

Manning the machine, Lawrence moved quickly. The skin on his hands was parched and scarred in various spots. They were working hands. He was milling a batch of yellow corn grits. I watched as he turned on the Meadows Mill stone-burr machine and poured a bucket of kernels into the funnel feeding into the mill. There was a loud *crunch* as the corn made its way between the stones, and the machine seemed to fight back, whirring louder as the quantity of grains increased. Lawrence pointed down to a small drawer at the bottom of the machine. It was slowly filling with a pile of corn dust and grits. Lawrence kneeled down to dip his fingers into the drawer and pinched at the powder. He stood up to show me what he was looking for.

"See that? It's coarse and we need it to be finer," he said, separating the minuscule pieces with his index finger from the larger, sesame seed–size chunks. He stopped the machine and pulled a lever, incrementally working the stones closer together. He turned it on again and I could hear a *whoosh* as the stones began to churn the kernels again. It sounded like teeth clenching as the corn moved between the stones.

Lawrence waited a few more minutes, then pulled out the drawer to test the fine powder once more. It was like a dance, this up-and-down motion, him swaying on his feet as he waited to see what the machine might produce. Again, the granules were too coarse, and again, he turned off the machine to adjust the distance between the stones. Up and down, rhythmically working the machine like he was milking a cow, he knelt and stood, the movement of his lanky limbs gentle.

After he'd gotten the milled product to the size he wanted, it was time to start sifting. He placed a stainless-steel bowl under the dropping point and let a few pounds of corn run through the mill. Once the entire funnel of corn had been emptied into the mill and the bowl held a small mountain of fine yellow powder, he turned off the machine for good and moved the bowl onto a nearby table, where he'd set a twelve-inch round metal sifter over another large stainless-steel bowl. He dropped a few scoopfuls of the milled corn on top of the sifter and, using both hands, began to forcefully and rhythmically shake the sifter over the empty bowl. His whole body got into the movement, starting with his stiff hands and wrists, and gyrating out through his tattooed arms and toward his shoulders and legs. He stood over the bowl, sifting, sifting, sifting, his muscles flexing with each shake.

He stopped for a moment and leaned over to pick up the hose of a commercial grade vacuum cleaner that sat beside him. I watched as he turned on the machine and held the edge of the hose just over the sifter. Like a stiff wind, the vacuum sucked up the wing-like white flecks that had risen to the top of the sifter.

"Pericarp," Lawrence shouted over the noise of the vacuum, referring to the tough, undesirable outer wall of the corn kernels, the part that might get stuck in your teeth when you're eating a handful of popcorn. In the milling process, the pericarp was separated from the endosperm and the germ, but millers like Lawrence, who were detail-focused and intent on product quality, took extra measures to separate it from the grits and ensure that it didn't wind up in the final product. Eccentric sifters, those vertical stacks of white boxes that gyrated to sift the meal, which I'd seen at Anson Mills, and the old horizontal version I'd seen at Geechie Boy, did this on a larger scale. But the vacuum removed even more of the unwanted little bits. It was an innovation on the practice that, long ago, involved simply tossing milled corn up in the air and letting the wind carry the finer pieces off.

I wondered how long it had taken Lawrence to learn the precise angle and distance at which to hold the vacuum hose—he kept it several inches from the surface of the corn and nothing but flaky pericarp seemed to get sucked up into the nozzle. How did he keep from sucking up the rest of the corn—and their profits along with it? Lawrence was watching me watching him.

He laughed, reading my mind: "It takes some practice."

He turned off the vacuum and continued sifting, adding more milled corn to the pile. He went through maybe a cup or two of the product at a time, proving how very time-consuming and physically intensive this gig could be. I remembered seeing several guys doing something similar at Anson. Here Lawrence and Ken were the only millers, and Congaree's product depended not only on his physical abilities but also on his skill with the machine, the sifter, and the vacuum. It was an art.

As Lawrence went through his routines, I turned to Ken to ask how business was going. Now three years into it, he said, they were both finally able to make this their full-time work. The first few years were tough. They'd started out milling at one facility, then made plans to open their own but got held up by permits. At the time, Ken was doing work for City Roots, an urban farm in town, and Lawrence was driving cabs and slinging pizzas at Dano's part-time—they approached the restaurant's owner, Dan Scheel, about using part of the kitchen space to mill in the mornings. Dan agreed to it, and he'd been a mentor ever since, Ken explained.

I probed more deeply—What was their demo? How much were they charging for their grits? Ken thought for a moment. He struggled sometimes with the cost of organic food production, he admitted. "When I go to these farmers' markets on the outskirts of town, I get a lot of old-timers, people who want fresh grits but don't want to pay eight dollars a pound. We charge five dollars, and still, some of them walk away shaking their heads," he explained. "When we're at Soda City—in the city, near campus— the price goes up," he added. "It covers our fee to be a vendor—but we also sell more there in a day than we do at all of the other markets combined in a week."

So it's important that they keep costs reasonable, he added, but also that they stick with an organic product—he was eager to get a USDA inspection so they could put the "certified organic" labeling on their products. "I have no interest in milling genetically modified corn," he added. "I realize I'm not going to change the world by making that choice. Maybe GMO corn is safe, but to me, the idea of someone eating proprietary information just boggles the mind."

Lawrence had wrapped up the batch of yellow quick grits he'd been working on and was ready to move on to the roasted corn, which he would mill for polenta. I asked what the difference was, in terms of the grind, and he said the grind they use for polenta would be even smaller than what they used for the quick grits, but that they would also mix cornmeal in with it, which would give the polenta a creamier consistency.

Mixing and blending the various grinds was part of a miller's skill set, too. Each miller might have a different ratio or method for mixing, ensuring that their end product held the right texture and consistency. The grits could be coarse without any meal, or a mix of coarse and fine, depending on a customer's preference. Chefs would request particular mixes depending on what they were using it for, too. For the roasted yellow corn polenta, Lawrence pulled out a bag of roasted cornmeal he'd milled the day before so he could create the blend as he was sifting.

I could tell the guys were ready to push on, so I yawned and started to make my exit, claiming a need for more coffee. Ken waved good-bye before turning to a bag of blue corn, which he would measure out and hand to Lawrence to run through the mill. It would be their last run of the morning.

After holing up at a Starbucks for an hour or so, I wandered over to the Gourmet Shop in downtown Columbia in search of breakfast. I found Ken sitting at a table outside, across from his son. He was eating an omelet. "Best way to end a morning at the mill." He smiled. Inside, I ran into Lawrence, who was talking to one of the Gourmet Shop's employees, Nate, the person who purchased their grits for the restaurant. I asked Nate which Congaree products they bought—and why.

"They brought in some samples early on, when they were just starting out. So we cooked up a batch and immediately said, 'Wow. These actually taste like corn,'" Nate said. Simple as that.

I couldn't leave Columbia without tasting some Congaree grits. That night, I found my way to the Oak Table, one of their best accounts. A handsome space wrapped in recovered barn wood, the restaurant had dark, moody lighting and a long, smooth wooden bar. It sat at the base of a tall office building, and looking out from my perch at the bar, I could see the state capitol across Gervais Street. It was lit up from the ground, making it appear calm and regal on that stormy night.

I watched as the wind picked up outside the window, whipping the treetops more and more violently as the night went on. The lone television in the space was showing a football game, but a scroll at the bottom of the screen announced various warnings about the oncoming storm. With a glass of Cabernet in hand, I felt safe in that wood-lined space, protected from whatever elements might be headed my way.

After snacking on an order of grilled corn, I surprised the

bartender by ordering a side of grits as my main dish. "Probably just the thing on a night like this." He smiled. A small black cast-iron dish arrived; inside, the grits were nestled in a mound with a few sliced scallions on top for garnish. The grits were large and pearled, almost like someone had taken hominy and folded it with a creamy white cheese.

The chef, Todd Woods, requested a custom grind for his grits, Ken had told me. "We brought a few variations and he tasted them all, but then asked us for the coarsest grind we could get—so that's what he orders, our coarsest grind with no other meal blended in," he said, speculating that the chef cooked them for about three hours to get them just right.

I dipped my fork in, marveling at the size of the kernel bits, which kept their structure despite being as smooth as cream. It was like eating a bowl of risotto—the corn had been cooked down to a luscious, creamy consistency that still managed to hold its toothy bite. I tasted both cheese and smoke underneath it all, but on top, there was the distinctly bright flavor of pure corn. I re-membered Ken's other tidbit about this dish: Chef Todd makes his own cheese and uses the whey when cooking his grits.

I sipped my wine and took another bite of the grits, trying hard not to wolf it down all at once. Though I loved wine and had a basic education in tasting and pairing, red wine and grits was a new one for me. I tried the two together again and the flavors mingled in that comforting, warm-sweater kind of way. These two seemingly opposing foods were, in fact, very similar in that both required the patient efforts of people to grow and harvest the plants, and then work their magic to process them in a way that preserved the flavor while creating a wholly new ingredient. I considered Sean Brock's comment about *terroir* and realized that regardless of what flavors I was getting from the grits, his comment certainly applied here: The grits, just like the wine, radiated a very specific sense of place.

I checked in on Ken and Lawrence periodically after my visit. In late 2017, Ken let me know that he'd bought Lawrence out of the business and that his former partner was now working at the Mueller's Pasta plant, just outside of town. "I guess milling is still a sort of calling for him," he said in an email.

I took it as a good sign, and hoped that both of them kept the tradition of small-batch milling alive in some way. And although the processing of corn had come a long way, and the colors of the faces and hands who worked the corn into grits had changed from predominantly brown and black to white (and mostly male), the fact remains that the resulting dish, which itself can come in myriad colors, now belongs to all of us.

BASIC BLACK SKILLET CORNBREAD

Courtesy of Kenneth DuBard, Congaree Milling Company

Serves 6 or more

2 cups cornmeal, plus more if needed

1 teaspoon salt

1 tablespoon sugar

1 tablespoon baking powder

½ teaspoon baking soda

1½ cups whole milk or heavy cream, plus more if needed

2 eggs

Preheat the oven to 450ºF. Grease a 14-inch cast-iron skillet and set it in the oven to preheat as well.

In a large bowl, whisk together the cornmeal, salt, sugar, baking powder, and baking soda until thoroughly combined.

In a separate large bowl, whisk together the milk and eggs until thoroughly combined.

While whisking, add the dry mixture to the wet and whisk until combined. If the batter isn't rather loose, add more milk. If the batter is too loose and watery, add more cornmeal a tablespoon at a time until it thickens to the desired consistency.

Carefully remove the hot skillet from the oven and pour in the batter—it should sizzle on contact. Return the skillet to the oven. Bake for about 20 minutes, or until golden brown and a toothpick inserted into the center of the cornbread comes out clean and dry.

Serve with butter, honey, or however you like.

NOTE: The recipe can be halved. A muffin tin can be used instead of a skillet (a tin does not need to be preheated) and the cooking time shortened to 12 to 15 minutes. You can also use ¼ cup sour cream or plain yogurt in place of ¼ cup of the milk or cream.

The True Grit-Slingers

How and *When* Southern Women Bring Grits to the Table

The connection between women and grits goes back as far as the origins of corn itself. From the Aztec's Centeotl to the Cherokee's Selu, goddesses in numerous cultures are known to be created from maize and to be the givers of maize to man.

"In Cherokee mythology of the southern Appalachians, the ancestral mother, Selu, bestowed the gift of corn on all Indian people of this era, and her name remains the tribal word for corn. Because a woman goddess gave birth to corn in native tradition, female tribe members continued this gendered labor and became the South's first intensive farmers," wrote Marcie Cohen Ferris in her book *The Edible South.*[12]

The torch was eventually passed along to the enslaved. On plantations and small farms across the American South, female grain grinders and hominy makers carried grits, a meal of nour-ishment and fuel, into the modern era.

Women were, for centuries, the grits bearers. They produced it from the ground up, growing and harvesting the grain, then further committing to the physical acts of processing the corn and cooking the grits before sharing the bowls with those they provided for.

And yet when it comes to contemporary grits culture, it's white men whose voices are loudest and whose work gets the most acknowledgment. When Glenn Roberts at Anson Mills and Greg Johnsman at Geechie Boy on the production side, and chefs like Sean Brock at Husk and Frank Stitt in Birmingham, Alabama, discuss, prepare, and serve grits, their efforts are showcased, writ-ten about, and elevated to stories of greatness. Those stories, while valid and essential for their efforts to push the dish forward, often take up a lot of space, and regularly drown out those of women whose accomplishments and efforts bear equal value.

The Torch Bearers

As an important American grit slinger, the Virginia country cook and food writer Edna Lewis would have had something to say about these male chefs and their prettified preparations of grits. In their book *The Gift of Southern Cooking*, Lewis's coauthor, Scott Peacock, noted how he, as a chef, watched grits become trendy in the 1980s as other chefs started preparing them with pesto or sun-dried tomatoes or lemongrass, while Miss Edna Lewis's response was, "People should really leave grits alone."[13] The recipe for old-fashioned creamy grits that follows her remark does essentially that—although some more devout grits purists might find fault with her adding milk *and* heavy cream to the recipe. Lewis also offers up a version of grits with shrimp paste, a recipe she learned in Charleston. The paste gets stirred into a bowl of hot grits, which imparts a coral color to the plate. She calls for it to be served with toasted bread, for either breakfast or supper. Long before Frank Stitt and Sean Brock gained notoriety for their elevated preparations of ground corn, there were women like Edna, doing the work to bring grits to the table.

It started with the indigenous women who carried, cultivated, and honored the culture of maize, and not only provided us with multiple varieties of corn but also, by carrying out the physically demanding process of nixtamalizing, grinding, and cooking that corn over live fire to produce bowls of hot gruel, sustained and fed their kin for thousands of years. That was long before these traditions were passed on to, and later taken ownership of by, the settlers.

There were the enslaved women who sat beside a hearth or stood over a stone-covered pit nurturing pots of ground corn and water. These captive black women pounded, stewed, and stirred pots of corn, water, and wood ash over fire for five or six hours in order to make hominy. Then they dried it and pounded it, once again using their own physical force to produce what would ultimately become fuel to power manual labor. Sometimes the mush was served like slop, in a trough or set on the floor for multiple hungry mouths to fight over. Other times, it was served on tables, though not ones set with silver and linen. This form of cooking was applied in the kitchen of the slave owner, too, so as time marches on, bowls of grits are passed from black hands to white ones, eaten by all. Some of these women had recipes that appeared in books written by white women—maybe they were named, but usually they were not. When African Americans finally did produce their own cookbooks, many of which have been collected and explored by the author Toni Tipton-Martin in her book *The Jemima Code: Two Centuries of African American Cookbooks*, grits were never included in the early recipe lists. Instead, those rare publications were filled with the dishes that had helped some of these women gain their independence.

There were the housewives of the 1920s, black and white, who could now buy their grits in a box. Once the hot corn porridge caught the eye of industrial cereal makers—Jim Dandy and Quaker—it was sold to home cooks as hot breakfast cereal that could be prepared quickly and effortlessly. Just after the First World War, these women were savvy about spending, pinching pennies in order to feed their families and likely stretching their boxes of grains as far as they could, using a little more water to thin out the dish.

Later, as those cereal brands grew in prominence, diversified their product lines, and expanded their reach across grocery store shelves and into the kitchens of Southern and Middle America, women used their resources to help other home cooks learn the joys of cooking with grits.

That's where home economics teachers like Linda Carman came in. Originally from Cullman, Alabama, Linda grew up the youngest of five children and learned to cook at her mother's side. She picked fresh blackberries to make into jelly and ate hot, crispy, thin corn bread, cooked quickly in a hot skillet coated in lard, which her mother would put in the oven when they spotted her father's green pickup coming down the hill.

Linda majored in home economics at Nashville's David Lipscomb College (now Lipscomb University), and stayed in Nashville after graduation. It was 1968, and at the time, a gas company was hiring home ec experts to go into home kitchens and teach women how to cook on their new gas stoves. Linda did that job for several years before she was asked to take over the test kitchen at Martha White, which at the time was attached to Royal Flour Mills, based in Nashville. By the time Linda came along, the test kitchen had been operating for nearly twenty-five years under Alice Jarman, who developed recipes, traveled the South, and taught kids in schools and adults in their home kitchens how to cook. Alice worked to develop a series of recipes that would utilize the brand's self-rising flour and cornmeal and handed them out on recipe leaflets. When Alice retired, she handed the kitchen reins to Linda, who worked for the brand for more than forty years.

As a brand ambassador for Martha White, Linda took to the roads, offering cooking demonstrations in women's home kitchens or at community town halls. Her skill was getting people comfortable around the stove or handling a dough or a batter while she talked directly and casually, doling out tips as she cooked. Along the way, she spread the gospel of Martha White, offering home cooks a personal link to the brand they'd reach for regularly at the grocery store.

In 1981, Martha White, which had merged with Beatrice Foods, purchased Jim Dandy, a well-known brand since the 1920s.

Linda was tasked with creating focus groups across the South to give the brand a better understanding of how women actually cooked and served their grits. During one group meeting, somewhere in the mountains of Georgia, Linda met an African American woman who lived out in the country. She told Linda how she had grown up very, very poor, and how her family had eaten grits when she was growing up. Her mother put a pot of grits on the stove in the morning, where they simmered all day long. The kids ate them if they needed a snack, and the family ate them with every meal. Her mother simply kept adding water to the pot and stirring them some more, which made the grits creamier and creamier. Linda believed that grits were a constant for this woman—an aching memory but also an essential one. Her family likely raised the corn themselves, taking it to a miller who ran a small water-powered mill along a stream. It was cheap fuel for a starving family, but also the glue that held them together, Linda believed.

A few years later, in 1986, Jim Dandy became one of the first sponsors of the World Grits Festival in St. George, South Carolina. Linda and her husband, as well as a few others who worked for Jim Dandy, went down to St. George every year for the festival—at least until someone from the corporate office decided Jim Dandy didn't need to be a sponsor anymore.

Around the same time the World Grits Festival was kicking off, Knoxville-based White Lily Flour (like Martha White, it's now owned by the J. M. Smucker Company) asked cook and culinary teacher Nathalie Dupree if she'd be interested in hosting a television show. Nathalie had already run her own restaurant, and started and oversaw a prominent cooking school inside Atlanta's Rich's department store. The show, *New Southern Cooking with Na-*

thalie Dupree, started airing on PBS in 1986 and led to Nathalie
filming nine different television series over the years.

At the time, Nathalie's "realistic" approach to cooking gave
viewers an honest side of home cooking—the smiling, straight-
forward blonde, wearing shoulder pads and a patterned apron,
might drop a pot or spill a sauce and respond with a casual shrug
and an "I bet that doesn't happen in your kitchen" smile. Her food
was real—she covered the basics, from crispy dinner rolls to potato soup, but also threw in tips for shucking oysters and piecing
together good pies. Grits were a major player in Nathalie's TV
meals. She recommended them for breakfast and dinner. Or with
greens, in custards, and as a soufflé paired with rosemary and
grapes. And, of course, she regularly served them, in variously
easy and complicated ways, as a bed for shrimp. (She eventually
published an entire book on the topic called *Nathalie Dupree's Shrimp
& Grits Cookbook*.)

At the time, Julia Child was the other recognizable female face
on television, but Nathalie's approach, using techniques that were
global but almost always with Southern ingredients, made an
impression on women who cooked just like she did: for ladies'
luncheons and church suppers, brunches and family meals.
The dishes Nathalie and her viewers made were to be set on tables
surrounded by family and used to fill and please loved ones—
and grits were right there in the middle of it all.

Nathalie's show, and her career as a food writer, helped spawn
the careers of many other grits-loving experts, including Virginia
Willis, who started as an apprentice of Nathalie's. Virginia went
on to pen her own cookbook about grits, this one for Short Stack
Editions, a collection of single-topic short-format recipe books. In

the introduction for the Short Stack grits book, Willis called herself a "grits missionary" and peppered a range of uses for grits throughout the pages, including them in recipes for soup, beignets, and congee.

But even as each of these women crafted and shared their recipes, and used their platforms to educate and pass grits dishes along, men spoke louder. The takeover started to occur in the late 1980s with chefs like Bill Neal, who gained attention for putting shrimp and grits into the greater American canon. The *New York Times* writer and editor Craig Claiborne uplifted stories like Neal's and those of other male Southern chefs of that era. As grits moved from home kitchens to cafés, and later into the white-tablecloth restaurants of the South, men took up more and more space in the grits story line. The result is that today, when grits are referred to in a recipe to cook at home, that recipe usually comes from a woman. But when they're offered on a menu, with a high ticket price and more ingredients than might seem necessary, they are presented by a man.

Exceptions exist, of course. Female restaurant chefs present grits in prettified ways more and more these days. At the Barn at Blackberry Farm, the revered luxury property set in Walland, Tennessee, executive chef Cassidee Dabney serves hers topped with a poached egg, its fleshy white exterior cut with a small incision to reveal a marigold-orangey yolk. Underneath, the creamy, yellowish-red grits mix with the egg yolk for a soothing and flavorful bite. Chef Katie Button, of Asheville, North Carolina, keeps a finely tuned Spanish focus at her restaurant Cúrate, but nearby at her other outpost, Nightbell, she makes hush puppies with grits, or folds them into the dough of a brioche bun that gets wrapped around a brandied beef.

And then there are those who are doing the simple work of putting grits on a plate for breakfast, or using them as the base for something heartier and more soul-filling at supper, and aren't getting accolades for it, even though they should. In a storefront café set deep in Savannah's Midtown neighborhood, you can find a solid plate of grits at a spot called Narobia's Grits & Gravy. In the tightly filled basic diner space, where red plastic cups hold your tea and a few fans spin lazily overhead, the crowd is democratically served. Orders are taken with a pat on the shoulder, and everyone seems to know everyone else. There, one can revel in the sounds of lip-smacking excitement that inevitably rise up with the arrival of a plate that groans from the weight of steaming, oozy grits smothered in a brown gravy and accented with big, plump, pink shrimp. Like a siren call, a deep-throated moan of joy often ripples across the room as plate after plate of grits, served humbly and with care, go out to feed the masses.

⟋Ꭷ⚹Ꭷ⟍

SWEET AND CREAMY GRITS

Serves 4

*Arguments abound on whether one should add sugar to their grits—
depending on where in the country you reside, you might balk or swoon at
the thought. Inspired by a sweetened grits cream recipe, I decided to try my
hand at adding sweetness to a dish of grits. The end result tastes like a
creamy corn pudding that you can eat for breakfast or late in the day as an
afternoon snack.*

1 cup stone-ground grits

1 cup milk

2 cups heavy cream, plus more if needed

2 tablespoons honey

¼ teaspoon salt

1 teaspoon vanilla extract

Fresh blueberries or peaches, sliced

In a heavy-bottomed pot, combine the grits, milk, cream, and honey.
Let sit for about 10 minutes, then place over medium heat. Bring the
mixture to a simmer, stirring frequently, then reduce the heat to low and
simmer, stirring occasionally, for 30 to 35 minutes, until the grits are
smooth and creamy. Add the salt and vanilla and stir to combine. If
the grits are too thick, stir in a bit more cream to thin them slightly.
Serve warm, topped with fresh blueberries or sliced peaches.

Hot Grits

Not all associations with grits and women are positive, though. Yes, the dish can be a salve, calming a hungry child, or, in some cases, even used directly on the body, rubbed onto the chest as a way to cure congestion. But, as I also came to learn, grits can evoke painful memories for many. Early in my research, I sat down with writer Alice Randall, author of *The Wind Done Gone*, and co-author, along with her daughter, Caroline Randall Williams, of the cookbook *Soul Food Love*. Alice avoided grits because of an experience she had with them at a young and observant age.

The story revolves around her African American grandmother, who was born in 1898 and started her first kitchen at the age of fifteen in Selma, Alabama. After World War II, the family migrated to Detroit, Michigan, where her grandmother served beautiful food that, it turned out, was usually prepared by her grandfather.

In Alice's world, the women of her family were strong figures, but it was her father who, in her mind, was all-powerful. He was the boss of her but also of the house, a man to be respected and adored. When she was a young girl, on a visit to her grandparents' home in Detroit, her grandmother cooked a dish of grits with liver and onions, mostly for Alice's father, who had eaten the dish growing up. Alice saw the plate and didn't want to eat it. There was a pool of rich and dark brown gravy running off the pile of grits. Alice told her father she did not want to eat it. Her father looked down at her and said, "You'll eat it because she is the boss of me."

Alice realized then that it wasn't her father, but her grandmother who was the greater authority which, at the time, was a shocking notion to her—it would forever alter the way she perceived her father. The experience traumatized her, she recalls. "After that, I literally never ate grits again until my thirties."

Today, Alice admits, she will make a form of grits with black-eyed peas. There's no corn involved, and she serves them in a martini glass with shrimp, but she says she still doesn't like the association they conjure for her.

Alice's story was a reminder that grits are not always comfort. In some cases, they're traumatic. Or even worse, used to cause pain. There are many stories that have come to light of how some people, women mostly, use grits as an actual weapon, with the hot grits inflicting body-altering pain—usually on a man.

One situation, involving musician turned reverend Al Green, takes the prize as the most striking and famous case of grits used as a weapon. In 1974, the pop singer was doused with a pot of scalding-hot grits while sitting in his bathtub in Memphis. Green shortly left the world of music behind and turned to a life of preaching—but the scars are likely still intact. The heat of boiling grits can cause second- and third-degree burns—or, when mixed with hot grease, inflict even worse injury. (That's just what happened in Orlando, Florida, in a 2014 incident. The attacker was charged with attempted second-degree murder.) Other cases have occurred all across the South—a woman in Louisiana hit her ex, who'd recently broken up with her, with a pot of grits while he slept; a Maryland resident poured hot grits on her man in bed before beating him with a baseball bat.

Julia Reed, the lively humor columnist, wrote in *Garden & Gun* about these examples and several more, saying that the act of flinging hot grits on another human "gives a whole new meaning to the term *packing heat* (not to mention *white-hot*)."

Dry, raw grits can cause equally grueling (ahem) moments of pain, such as the one portrayed in the fictional 2003 coming-of-age drama *The Secret Life of Bees*, written by Sue Monk Kidd. The author wrapped up an emotionally mobilizing moment for the main character, Lily, who was forced to kneel on an anthill-size pile of coarse, dry Martha White grits for an hour as punishment for sneaking out of the house. The "powdered-glass feeling" caused Lily's skin to welt and bruise.

Whether used by or on women, or simply as a signifier of power, grits can leave deep scars—ones that can't be comforted with a spoon and a bowl.

The Reclamation

After meeting the male millers behind Congaree and Anson, I went searching for any female faces I could find who might be working stone mills to make grits. The first one I found was at Geechie Boy—it was Betsy Johnsman's sister, Katie. After our walk through the market, Betsy took me over to the milling room, set a few hundred feet away, and introduced me to Katie, who had learned to mill from Greg Johnsman; she was now doing the bulk of the milling for the company. Greg handled many of the specialty grains, fulfilling orders that required a more specialized milling technique. But for most of their product, Katie worked off a larger mill built in 1962 that was attached to a long, silver separator that the team called the Silver Bullet. It had come from a woman in Florida whose father had owned it—she wanted it to have a good home when he passed way. Greg had rebuilt the interior mechanisms, including putting different gauges of wire screen into the separator, which allowed them to provide varying levels of coarseness to their grits and meal. Geechie Boy sold their products to several dozen restaurants and through various retail operations, including their own market, as well as through their online retail store.

The day I was there, Katie was milling a little bit of Jimmy Red corn, an heirloom grain that had recently gotten a lot of attention for the efforts being made to bring it back from near extinction. Because so little of it had thrived over the years, Geechie Boy's allotments were minimal and batches only went out bit by bit.

The mill itself sat at one end of a large barn that also had an adjoining cold storage space. A massive funnel-like hopper was set above the mill. I watched as Katie hauled a five-gallon bucket up toward her shoulder and slowly poured the bright red kernels of Jimmy Red into the funnel. The loud *whir* of a fan-driven blower pushed the milled grains from between the turning millstones into the long, silver separator. One of the chamber doors of the separator was open, and I could see the final ground product, a fine shower of reddish dust, dropping down from the screen.

The room was remarkably tidy. Katie, in a green apron, jeans, Crocs, and a medical-grade white face mask, moved deliberately but without rushing. At one point, I saw her lay her hand on the side of the mill, feeling its external temperature.

"She knows that machine inside and out—she can tell just by the smell whether it's running all right. She knows what to listen for, what to feel for," Betsy explained. The mill could churn through several hundred pounds at a stretch before it needed a break, at which point Katie would turn the machine off and give it time to cool down.

As I had with Lawrence Burwell, I could see Katie's movements fall in step with the machine's. Though my visit was brief, it encouraged me that there might be more women like her, who used both skill and intuition to produce today's small-batch grits.

※

Georgeanne Ross greeted me in her green pickup truck at the end of the long drive that led to a hidden-away warehouse and milling space near Oxford, Mississippi. About five feet tall, with a trim frame, Georgeanne had a head of white hair cropped short so that it just curled around her forehead. Her broad smile and quiet, throaty laugh welcomed me as we drove the short, unpaved distance to her mill.

I'd found Georgeanne through her website—she called herself the Original Grit Girl, and although she didn't seem to be selling her grits to many retail outlets, I'd found references to her grits at various restaurants around Oxford, including City Grocery, owned by James Beard Award–winning chef John Currence. At the upscale Oxford restaurant Snackbar, chef Vishwesh Bhatt sometimes used Original Grit Girl grits folded together with coconut milk, ginger, and vegetables to make a version of the Indian dish kanji.

As Georgeanne and I bumped along the lane toward her property, she told me about her husband, Freddie, who had passed away about a year back. Her voice lowered as she spoke—it was still hard for her to talk about. "All of this started with him," she said as we pulled up alongside a bright-red metal storage facility. "He loved to tinker, so he collected all these old machines. That's what got me into this whole thing," she added. "Honestly, I just kind of fell into it."

We walked inside to find her milling operation, which consisted of two old mills and a white steel Meadows Mills grits bolter. My eye immediately set upon a red antique mill that was hooked up to the separator via long metal tubing. "That's an original Meadows." Georgeanne beamed. It was built by Mr. Meadows himself, she claimed. It had been found years ago, discarded out in a field somewhere. Her husband had restored it and worked with a nearby millstone dresser, one of the only people in the area who still did the work by hand, to cut and sharpen the stones.

"I call her my grit bitch," Georgeanne said, nearly doubling over with a laugh.

This was actually Georgeanne's second go at being a miller. She'd launched her first business, called Delta Grind, around 1999, almost, as she says, by accident. She'd been a bookkeeper for more than twenty years when she met Freddie, who was a share-cropper raising cotton and soybeans. Freddie had an interest in repairing old machines. A friend had gifted him an old flywheel engine, so he fixed it up and attached it to an antique gristmill.

"He wanted to show me where cornmeal came from," she said, adding that after that first demonstration, the two started milling at home once a month or so. Georgeanne usually gave the meal away, bringing it up to her family members who lived in Memphis, including a brother who owned a few bars in the area. At some point along the way, the cornmeal landed in the hands of a Memphis chef. "He said, 'I've got a list of six other chefs that want fresh meal, and you're the only one making it,'" she explained. After a little convincing, she decided to try her hand at the business, targeting white-tablecloth restaurants around Memphis, Oxford, and Tupelo—after a year, she gave up her bookkeeping to work full-time on the milling operation. Soon she had about sixty restaurants buying from her regularly, including those owned by John Currence.

In 2008, the miller's life came to a halt when Georgeanne's mother had a stroke. "I just needed to focus," she said, so she sold the business to a young woman named Becky Tatum, who was part of a prominent family in Oxford.

Georgeanne eventually got through her own personal struggles, and in the meantime, John Currence had started calling to ask if she might consider milling again. "He called me for a year," she said, smiling. "He said, 'I'll take everything you can mill.'"

Finally, she caved, asking John for about three months so she could get another mill running. Freddie, who by now had acquired a few more of the old machines, got to work restoring the "grit bitch," and soon Georgeanne was milling corn again, this time exclusively for John and his restaurants. As other chefs caught wind that she was grinding again, she was able to restart the business, this time as the Original Grit Girl. Her sales list grew to more than 160 accounts, with a few retailers included in the mix this time around, and her products now included grits, polenta, and cornmeal.

From the get-go, Georgeanne used a yellow field corn from a regional distributor called Ware Milling, based in Houston, Mississippi, which received its corn from a co-op of nearby farmers. The corn came in large, 50-pound bags and the kernels had all been cleaned—but Georgeanne also sent the corn through her own cleaner before grinding it in the mill. "I am really picky and I stay on 'em when the corn isn't clean. I'll go down there and raise hell if the bags are full of dirt," she said. She ran her business like a no-nonsense ship's captain, demanding perfection from herself and her suppliers.

When she first started buying from the co-op in 2000, the cost of a 50-pound bag was $1.50. Seventeen years later, it was up to $9.25. "And I only just raised my prices this past year," she admitted—just 50 cents per pound wholesale.

Georgeanne's business ran like clockwork. She'd call her restaurants and take their orders every other Friday; she then milled the following Sunday, a process that took about four hours, starting at seven a.m., then she'd mill a few more buckets on Tuesday. The shipments would go out on Wednesdays. During the off weeks, she would mill again on Tuesdays to fill any additional orders. She wanted to ensure that her restaurants had fresh meal, grits, and polenta coming in about every two weeks—and she communicated with them regularly to make sure they weren't over-ordering. "That's the bookkeeper in me—there's no sense in ordering too much when I'm going to call you in nine days with more. I want to keep it fresh," she explained.

Although Georgeanne had been building up her business a bit more after Freddie passed away, she admitted that she was starting to tire of all the lifting. Her milling process involved the help of three others—two men and another woman. "We divide the room, so the guys run the mill and haul the corn, and we fill and measure the bags," she said. "It's guys versus girls—but we're usually waiting on them to keep things moving." She laughed. Still, the process could be taxing, especially because everything would get shipped from Georgeanne's own house, which meant transporting the goods from this property to her home, several miles away on the other side of town.

The woman she'd hired was actually an apprentice, she explained. Brittany Barnes, who also ran a seed supply store and nursery in town where Georgeanne bought her corn, had expressed interest in watching Georgeanne mill a few years back. Since then, Brittany had been slowly learning the trade, helping Georgeanne with the mill, and was now learning the back end of the business, too. When Freddie died, Brittany offered to buy the business. "I said, I'll do this as long as I can, as long as I'm physically able," Georgeanne recalled. "But eventually, I'm looking forward to passing it on to her. I want to keep it with the girls, you know?"

I asked how that had gone, running this business as a woman and navigating the male-dominated industries—kitchens, food production, delivery, agriculture. She was the only woman out there most days, she said. Even the delivery folks for operations like Sysco were all men. She laughed, recalling a moment when, very early in her business, her husband had encouraged her to wear fake boobs when heading out on sales calls. "I did it once and had six accounts come in that day," she hooted. After a pause, she added with a world-weary shrug, "It just goes to show what that world is really like."

Georgeanne's business came up at an important time in the Oxford food scene. When City Grocery opened in the early '90s, it was pretty much the only restaurant in town doing white-tablecloth food made from local ingredients. Otherwise, the Square wouldn't see much in the way of fine-dining or thoughtful food for decades, and only recently had the town seemed to come into its own as young guns, many of whom got their start at one of John Currence's restaurants, had started opening more progressive spots. There was a restaurant called Grit in nearby Taylor, whose hallmark grit cake was made with Original Grit Girl products, and Saint Leo, a polished yet casual Italian restaurant that served up pizzas and small plates made from local ingredients, as well as finely made cocktails.

While Georgeanne had managed to keep a lot of the restaurants on the Square as customers, she'd also started to travel beyond Memphis and Oxford to pick up new business, including down to Hattiesburg and Gulfport, where she had someone selling her grits at the local farmers' market.

But part of her reason for picking up new business was motivated by renewed competition in town. Mostly, this was thanks to the business she originally started, Delta Grind, which was getting new legs under a new owner, plus others, like Anson Mills, which was supplying specialty products that Georgeanne didn't want to mess with. Still, the Original Grit Girl was going strong—and would keep doing so as long as Georgeanne had her hand on the business.

༄჻༄

ORIGINAL GRIT GIRL GRITS AND VEGETABLE KANJI

Courtesy of Chef Vishwesh Bhatt

Serves 6 to 8

"Feel free to add a poached or fried egg, if you like. And change up the vegetables based on what you have on hand."

3 tablespoons clarified butter or oil

1 teaspoon mustard seeds

1 teaspoon cumin seeds

2 small shallots, minced

2 tablespoons minced fresh ginger

2 cups Original Grits Girl grits

1 serrano pepper or jalapeño, minced

½ cup diced carrots

½ cup diced cauliflower

½ cup green peas

½ cup diced tomatoes

6 cups chicken or vegetable stock

1 cup unsweetened coconut milk

½ cup roasted peanuts

¼ cup chopped fresh cilantro

Zest and juice of 1 lime

½ teaspoon ground turmeric

4 tablespoons (½ stick) butter

Salt and freshly cracked black pepper

In a heavy-bottomed pan, heat the clarified butter over low heat. Add the mustard seeds and heat until they start popping. Add the cumin seeds and stir until fragrant. Add the shallots and ginger and cook until soft.

Add the grits and stir until they are evenly toasted. Add the remaining vegetables, the stock, and the coconut milk. Bring to a simmer and cook, stirring continuously, until the grits start to thicken. Stir in the peanuts, cilantro, lime zest, lime juice, and turmeric and cook until the grits are nice and soft but not mushy and all the vegetables are cooked through.

Remove from the heat, stir in the butter, and season with salt and pepper before serving.

Curious about how two small mills, both female-run, could exist in this tiny, tight-knit corner of Mississippi, I set up a time to get to know Delta Grind, and to learn about the similarities and differences between the two businesses.

It wasn't the oversize T-shirt she wore, or her long, tousled hair pulled up in a loose ponytail. It wasn't the neatly manicured nails, or that she was wearing mascara. No, what struck me about Julia Tatum, the current owner and operator of Delta Grind, which produced grits in Water Valley, Mississippi, was that she was wearing braces. If the casual air and Converse sneakers hadn't given away her twenty-six years, those clear, teeth-straightening devices revealed all.

I found Julia at her warehouse facility, about thirty minutes south of Oxford, on a Saturday afternoon. She was sweeping. "I'm a stickler about keeping this place clean," she said by way of introduction, her Mississippi drawl pulling her words out like a string of taffy. Surely, I thought, being a neat freak would deter someone from milling grain into a fine dust every single day—but Julia insisted that cleanliness was what kept her sane as she went about her business.

She walked me into her facility, where I could see that everything had been tidily put in its place. The huge, open room was uncluttered and organized. Aside from a few stainless-steel tables set at the center, the only major pieces of equipment were a large, 30-inch vertical stone burr Meadows mill, as well as a long, boxy, white grits bolter, just like the one I'd seen at Georgeanne's. Small rooms off to the side acted as an office and storage space—the shelving in there was packed full with white paper Delta Grind–branded bags, waiting to be filled with Julia's grits, polenta, cornmeal, and masa.

Around 2008, Georgeanne had sold Delta Grind to Julia's cousin-by-marriage, Becky. Becky and her husband, John, a chef, took on Delta Grind enthusiastically—but when Becky became a mom, the business took a back seat. Running a mill operation with two toddlers underfoot became more of a challenge than the Tatums could invest time into. When Becky announced in 2016 that she was going to sell the business, Julia stepped in.

Having graduated from the University of Mississippi with a degree in graphic design, Julia's first job was working for a marketing firm in Oxford. She quickly realized she wasn't satisfied—what she really wanted to do was work with her hands. Becky gave her that opportunity. "Everyone I knew loved Delta Grind grits.

And I could see that Becky's heart wasn't in it anymore—but I just couldn't let it fall apart," she explained. With little more than an initial $1,000 investment and plans to let the operation pay for itself, she took the mill over from her cousin.

Though she'd trained with Becky for about a month, always at night after putting in a full day at the marketing firm, she took over the business with very little experience actually operating the machinery. Plus, she still had her day job. A few months later, she was able to quit the marketing firm and take up milling full-time.

It took her only a minute to find her footing. She started by running the business the way it had been run by her cousin, which meant she was milling once every two weeks and delivering product to restaurants around Oxford and in Jackson and Memphis. But Julia soon spotted inefficiencies with the model—not enough product on the off weeks, too much driving around—and set about streamlining the process. Now she was milling one or two times a week and filling orders weekly. And instead of running over to Jackson or Memphis to make her own deliveries, she was shipping her product through UPS.

As the sole operator, Julia was wearing every hat: chief miller, salesperson, distributor, marketer. From taking orders and calling on customers to securing her corn, milling the product, bagging it up, and prepping it to ship, she had her hands on every part of the process—just as Georgeanne did over at the Original Grit Girl.

Julia was also putting her marketing and graphic design skills to use—she'd recently updated Delta Grind's branding and packaging, and was about to embark on designing a new website for the business in order to create a more formal online store. There were T-shirts in the pipeline, and perhaps other products, like cheese straw or cornbread mixes. This is where I saw Julia's youth working in her favor. Already she was looking to grow the business to fit with the landscape—customers, who were well-versed in farmers' market offerings and supporting local food sources, also wanted beautiful packaging and a convenient online store. Julia's understanding of the way she, as a modern retailer, could package both her story and her grits spoke to a generational power play, one that would keep her business afloat and likely push her milling operation in new and exciting directions.

Though she'd never milled before taking over the business, Julia was no stranger to working with heavy machinery. Her mother owned rental properties, she explained. She'd taught Julia to be her own handywoman. The two would often lay hardwood or tile together. "I know my way around a web saw," she said beaming. Plus, there was her mother's family farm, a three-thousand-acre property planted with corn.

"I've grown up around this product, so it's all familiar to me," she explained. "People will ask, 'You didn't do all of that yourself, did you?' And I'm like, do you see anyone else in here?"

I appreciated Julia's passion for the work—and her casual confidence, which gave me the impression that she believed there was absolutely no reason for anyone to question her capabilities. Her self-assurance was rock solid—she was pushing the business forward with nothing but positive energy and a commitment to the work itself.

What struck me, too, was her appreciation for the equipment. In buying the business, she'd purchased the mill and the separator,

both large, older pieces of machinery that required an engineering mind and tinkering hands to keep up. She did have help from
a man she called Mr. Eddie, an aging farmer who'd been coming
around to help with the equipment or on days when she was milling. He had helped her move the separator up onto a tall metal
frame so she could slide white, food-grade buckets underneath to
catch her product. They'd also updated the screens within the separator, which Julia said would make her milling process a little
more efficient.

I noticed another mill tucked away in the corner. "I really want
to get that one working again, too," she said, her eyes firing up.
Becky had been using it to mill wheat at one point, but Julia
wanted to restore it and use it to mill other grains, in the hopes of
further expanding her product line.

Julia claimed that her love of antique pieces came partly from
the fact that, growing up, she spent a lot of time with her grandmother Dorothy Lee Tatum, who lived in the antebellum home
Ammadelle, which sits near Oxford's main square. The home had
been filled with antique pieces, some of which were original to the
home. "When I was a kid, I didn't get it. I saw all this old stuff
and said, 'I want to live in a house with white furniture.' But now
I can appreciate where things came from and how we can bring
them back to use.'"

I did some research on Ammadelle after meeting Julia and
quickly came to understand that the home, which had been designed and built during the Civil War, had been a symbol of
wealth and stature for all who owned it. It had been constructed,
though, by the hands of enslaved black laborers. And the home
itself was also said to have harbored Confederate soldiers.

Julia hadn't mentioned any of this. Instead, she spoke proudly of the family's former ownership of the home, which had recently been sold (her grandmother passed away in 2015). She even teared up slightly, saying she couldn't talk about it because of how much history it held for her family.

I could tell that despite coming from a place of privilege, Julia had a deeply instilled work ethic—one that was driving her to push herself and her abilities, and to push her business in new ways.

For my visit, Julia had filled the working mill with three bushels of corn so she could demonstrate her process. The vertical, stone-burr Meadows was set inside a creamy white box that gleamed—Julia had taken impeccable care of the machine since purchasing the business.

I looked over to a pile of bagged corn—the same brand that Georgeanne used, all in 50-pound bags. Those bags weren't easy to haul, and I imagined that Julia was likely tossing a dozen or so on her shoulder every time she milled. There was also the packing and shipping—she laughed as she recalled her first UPS pickup. A man came knocking and, acting friendly, asked her who moved all those boxes out in front of the building for her. He didn't believe her when she told him. Her willowy frame belied the strength that resided deep down inside her.

She had, she admitted, added a few labor-saving techniques to her process, such as raising the separator high off the ground and putting her tall, food-grade buckets on rollers, making it easier to maneuver them around the warehouse. These efficiencies had allowed her to pick up the pace of the business and produce more grits to sell.

After teaching herself how to set the mill and watching her separator at work, Julia had come to understand her yields, and how to package her product according to the size of the granules she was getting. Running the corn through the mill on a single setting (i.e., without moving the stones), she could get plenty of masa (cornmeal flour), polenta, and grits with one run. She also made a coarse cornmeal by hand-mixing the masa with the polenta.

The grits had the highest demand, she said, but she was making a go at the masa, too—a tougher sell, since most restaurants or chefs who used masa were Mexican and already had their preferred brands imported. And the polenta, she admitted, was only polenta because of the size of the granules she was separating them by—true polenta, she admitted, was traditionally made with a different kind of corn. "People rarely know the difference around here, though, so I make it work," she said sheepishly. If there was any leftover product, including the chaff that would blow off the corn after it was ground or excess corn flour, she would leave it out in bags for local hog farmers to feed to their herds.

Although Julia appreciated the quality of the corn she was getting, she was ready to move in a new direction—she wanted to start sourcing a non-GMO variety. Ware Milling Company's yellow field corn usually arrived clean, she said, just as Georgeanne had. But Julia felt like she needed something to set her apart from her competition—a sticker reading "non-GMO" on her product labels would do just that. She'd already connected with a farmer based a little farther north, close to the Arkansas border, who was growing a few non-GMO varieties. Her plan was to switch to his product in a few months.

"Not only will it help differentiate me from everyone else out there, but I just think it's important—people are looking to get away from GMO varieties for a lot of different reasons," she said.

Her decision had come after some research—she'd been reading a few books on maize and was developing her own opinions about GMO varieties. From the starch content, which could affect the grind and the cooked results of the corn once it was prepared, to the environmental hazards of overplanting genetically modified products, her reasons for switching were clear. Plus, it could be a game changer for her business.

Were there heirloom varieties she wanted to try? I asked. She nodded, but said she needed to do more research. But the question of what color corn she would use was a nonstarter. "I'm just a yellow corn kind of girl." She smiled. "Grits is supposed to be yellow. When some people see white, all they think of are instant," she added—a sentiment shared by her main competitor.

I considered Julia and Georgeanne, two women at opposing ends of the spectrum in terms of age, wisdom, and experience, and saw that despite their differences, they were equals in the milling game. Where Georgeanne relied on consistency and word of mouth, Julia embraced evolution and modern marketing tools. Both felt the history of their work living alongside them, but not as a cloak under which they were smothered. Rather, by preserving a piece of the past—in both cases, the mills themselves—they had the right tools to help push them forward. Seeing both of these women-led businesses making grits—driven by the product as much as the machinery they so loved—and thriving in the heart and soils of Mississippi gave me hope for the future of small-batch, artisanal milling, and for the future of female millers.

※

While milling was an obvious place to look for female faces, another that didn't seem obvious to me at first was women who were growing the corn. In the long, unbroken tradition of Native American cultures, women were the primary seed-savers and preservationists. Women were the agriculturalists and the providers. Women were often the land "owners," too, the stewards who cared for the crops and the soil, sometimes maintaining the same lands for many generations.

In that vein, I set off in search of female farmers. There was Susana Lein, owner of Salamander Springs Farm near Berea, Kentucky, who was growing permaculture organic foods on ninety-eight acres in the Appalachian forest. She was using no-tillage and biodynamic practices, and her corn was grown with the three-sisters polyculture technique of growing beans, squash, and corn together in the same field. I came across a bag of her grits at the Berea farmers' market one Saturday morning—freshly milled, they were nearly bursting with corn flavor and seemed to come alive as they mingled with boiling water.

Other dedicated female farmers like Susana kept cropping up in my search, but I also found that there are a few who had been given a special type of platform, one that celebrated the "Southern artisan" spirit that these women seemed to signify. The most notable was Jennifer Nicely, whose family had been farming in Strawberry Plains, Tennessee, about thirty minutes northeast of Knoxville, for four generations. I first read about Jennifer in a magazine article published by the Charleston-based glossy, *Garden & Gun*. The piece featured the family prominently, using styled, modern-day farm-girl imagery that painted a rosy portrait of a twenty-first-century return-to-your-roots Southern farming family.

The Nicely property sits in a crook of the Holston River; Jennifer's grandfather James Nicely purchased the eight hundred acres in the early 1940s. Eventually, he had to lease or sell off parcels of the land, but the family still owned and farmed about four hundred acres. When Jennifer and her sisters were young, the farm served as a working dairy. The family had four hundred head of Holstein cattle in the high times—but by the late '80s, when a surplus of dairy was putting operations their size out of business left and right, the dairy went under. For three decades after the dairy closed, the Nicelys leased out the land, mostly to commercial tomato farmers.

Though Riverplains Farm still officially belonged to their father, Frank Nicely, a Republican who sat on the Tennessee state senate, Jennifer and her two sisters, Anna and Rachel, had come back to the farm to help steward the land in various ways.

Jennifer returned to Riverplains in 2009, after living abroad and later trying her hand as a singer and songwriter in Nashville. Anna, her younger sister, had already returned with her husband, Dino, after they'd learned that he was struggling with health issues. Anna and Jennifer came together, partnered with a family friend, Misty, and started a small business selling farm-raised products—dairy, cattle, eggs. Jennifer had the idea to start growing Hickory Cane corn.

The open-pollinated heirloom variety (which is identical to a variety called Hickory King) was far different than the GMO silage her father and uncles once grew to feed their dairy cattle.

But Jennifer, who had done some research, insisted that this would be a better way to use the land—they would stop using GMO products and grow as organically as possible, in an attempt to turn their land back into a healthy, sustainable space. It took some convincing, but eventually, they got Frank to agree, after helping him understand that growing organically wasn't new wave—it was the way the girls' grandfather had always done it.

Jennifer, Anna, Misty, Frank, and the farm were all on display in that lengthy *Garden & Gun* article. The piece shaped an idyllic and promising, if challenging, way of life for the family. But a few years after it was published, Jennifer was frustrated: Despite the glowing press, the girls' farm-to-table business, which included a food truck called Mister Canteen, wasn't working out.

"I think one of my mistakes, if I could call it that, was that I wasn't thinking big enough," Jennifer explained to me. I'd driven out to see her family's farm and we were jostling down along the river's edge in her white SUV. She had one sleeveless arm hanging out the driver's side window and wisps of hair blowing across her forehead.

"I was coming from a culinary perspective, you know? Wanting to raise products—whether it was an animal or a vegetable—that I really thought were the best, in a culinary sense. But apparently those always yield less and are more particular, take longer . . . it became a contradiction to try to compete with hybrid versions of everything."

She'd gotten a solid grits operation off the ground for a little while, using the Hickory Cane, which she believed might have been grown on the property before settlers arrived. (A fish trap, built from stones, still stretches across part of the river near the property—the family has dated it back to the 1500s.) She also tried a Wapsie Valley corn one season, but the two varieties crossed, so she decided to stick with just one single variety. To finish the product, she was driving it over to Valentine Mill, a historic facility from the 1800s that was a good hour-long drive from the farm. All that effort resulted in some delicious grits, though. "People told me they were the best they'd ever eaten, so fresh, good flavor," she said. "And they were consistent . . . but not as consistent as they could have been if I had control over every part of the process."

Her situation was conflicted. After the good press and a seemingly growing interest from consumers for local, sustainable food systems, surely there was a market for the grits, the eggs, the food truck—all of it. Plus, a pound of her grits was only $6.50 at the local health co-op. If there was an audience for Blackberry Farm, that top-rated luxury resort that sat just an hour down the road, surely there should be an audience for Riverplains Farm grits.

But it just wasn't working. "A lot of restaurants say they can't afford it. Eggs, grass-fed beef—I've encountered it with all our products. Most restaurants can't justify paying what you, as a small producer, need to make it even remotely worth your while. It's frustrating. But the bigger issue is that you can get all this attention for being a small, local producer—and people just think that you're living this idyllic life, somehow existing financially off of the products that you have. But you know, if no one is buying them, then you can't really justify it. It's like the system is not quite there."

The family was still growing Hickory Cane—they'd recently

contracted with a new customer, an up-and-coming distillery called Knox Whiskey Works. When I visited, the crop that was coming up would be one of the first to go to the distillery—an example of a partnership between corn grower and whiskey maker, which seemed to be gaining steam in the New South.

I asked if Jennifer was ready to give up on it all, including the grits. She replied that what she really wanted was to make a big investment—maybe get a mill for the farm, or put in some more infrastructure so she would have an easier time selling the product. She would keep at it, she said, smiling. "I mean, this"—she gestured out toward the four hundred acres surrounding us— "will always be here, right? We've got to carry it on for the next generation, too."

Because of her, and all the women who were now producing grits, that final thought resonated with me. Unlike the many male voices that had gained attention for themselves and boosted their own names, the women I met were quietly pushing forward—not in forceful, ego-driven ways, but rather with a confident yet guarded advance. As these women carry the skills, seeds, and, yes, preparations for grits forward, they do it to nourish, to sustain— and for the assurance that there will be more for many generations to come.

Political Grits

A Recipe for the Makings
of a Weapon—and a Tool

In April 2017, a small, conservative corner of the Internet lit up after a comment posted by a Fox News columnist claimed that President Barack Obama had "banned grits in Southern schools." The writer, Todd Starnes, propped up his argument using quotes from a child nutrition director in Alabama who complained that the 2010 Healthy, Hunger-Free Kids Act put in place by the Obama administration had removed all foods that weren't made with 100 percent whole grains from school cafeterias—and in Alabama schools, the grits were not whole-grain, but rather half whole-grain, a product likely produced by a cereal maker like Quaker using industrial, steel roller methods. (The flour the schools used to make biscuits was no longer compliant,

either, which became yet another sticking point for the nutrition director.)

Just a few months into Donald Trump's presidency, a delega-
tion of school nutritionists, including the one quoted, went to Congress to inform politicians of the issue, which is what prompted
Starnes to rail about it online, calling it a "war of culinary aggression."

Starnes's argument wasn't without its merits. Even the School
Nutrition Association, a trade group that represents tens of thousands of school food professionals—and, notably, suffers from its
own internal ethics debate, as its top donors include General Mills
and PepsiCo—was lobbying to have some stipulations of the
Healthy, Hunger-Free Kids Act pulled back. But to say that grits
had been "banned" was not entirely accurate. If, say, the Alabama
school system had been using stone-ground grits with no additives,
their ingredients might have passed the act's compliance test. But,
school budgets being what they are, efficiency being a necessity
of any school cafeteria, and kids having the palates that they do
(one report noted that children balked at the "black flecks" found
in the compliant "whole grain grits"), the industrially produced
half-whole-grain grits were likely that school district's only option.

A Presidential Dish

Still, this wasn't the first time someone had used grits as a political weapon. In fact, grits have been pulled into countless political
battles, both presidential and otherwise—most memorably with
the ascension of President Jimmy Carter.

Carter grew up in Plains, Georgia, eating grits regularly. The family didn't grow their own corn, or mill their own grits, but his mother, Lillian Gordy Carter, who went by Miss Lillian and stood on her own merits thanks to her work with the Peace Corps in India, raised her four children by putting grits on the table during breakfast, lunch, and dinner. In one of several cookbooks published at the time that showcased the Carter family and Plains, Georgia, called *Miss Lillian and Friends: The Plains, Georgia, Family Philosophy and Recipe Book*, there were recipes for grits 'n' greens, which called for white hominy grits; a cheese grits casserole, using quick grits; and a hominy recipe that suggested using one "No. 2 can white hominy."

As Jimmy Carter, a Georgia peanut farmer, made his way through the campaign cycle, his Southern roots and eating habits were widely discussed and dissected. When he attached himself formally to his vice presidential running mate, Walter Frederick Mondale, Carter became the "Grits" to Mondale's "Fritz," launching the popular button slogan "Grits & Fritz in '76."

After winning the presidency and settling into the White House, Carter, his wife, Rosalynn, and daughter, Amy, were gifted a dog, which happened to share a birthday with the date Carter was elected. Named Grits, the dog lasted in the White House for just a short while—when Grits's mother passed, the mutt was sent back to the teacher who'd originally gifted the dog to the Carters in consolation.

Southerners reveled in the many ways that Carter encouraged the presence of grits (the dish *and* the dog) in the White House and elsewhere. (Carter's staff even stashed bags of grits on Air Force One.) Others, meanwhile, gleefully mocked it. A cartoon that ran through the Tribune Media Services around the time of the inauguration showed two flummoxed White House chefs reading over the "Kitchen Transition" list. A deliveryman carrying three cartons of grits appears in the background to deliver the punch line: "Another load of grits, fellas. Where's it go? . . . Fellas? . . . Hey!"

Grits were, indeed, regularly served at the Carter White House. After a bit of instruction from Rosalynn, White House executive chef Henry Haller prepared them on the first morning the Carters took up residence and then regularly for visiting guests, Southern or otherwise. And, as Haller wrote in *The White House Family Cookbook*, "most were pleasantly surprised to discover they actually liked the taste of the ground hominy dish." Haller went on to explain that in order to make the grits "palatable," one needed to avoid a "watery product by cooking completely and stirring often." He also wrote about the fact that Rosalynn considered grits to be fattening—but he still served them every weekend, usually baked with cheese, which was the president's favorite style.

Meanwhile, grits were also crashing into the greater collective American consciousness during those years. Shortly after Carter won the Democratic nomination, Craig Claiborne reported in *The New York Times* that grits were being sold nationwide, noting that he'd found a box in the Hamptons. In November 1976, both the Quaker Oats Company and Jim Dandy saw a rise in sales of their grits products after what had been a short slump. By 1976, annual sales of grits had surged to more than $25 million nationwide.

Even so, a journalist writing in the *Los Angeles Times* felt inclined to spell out the definition of and uses for grits, saying they were made from "whole, dried white corn kernels that are degerminated and hulled as they pass through rollers." (As evidenced by his note that it was "white corn," he seemed to be specifically referencing the grits made by larger cereal producers, who only made grits from this type of corn.)

A year into Carter's presidency, Quaker Oats hosted a buffet-style "Great Grits Gala" at New York's Tavern on the Green, serving mushrooms stuffed with grits, garlic grits, and even grits mixed with caviar.

Despite the hoopla, a few pointed out that this was not the first time grits had been served inside the walls of the White House. This was Washington, DC, after all, a Southern-minded mid-Atlantic city where cooks, both black and white, had long fed world leaders and their families. The White House had, of course, been previously occupied by Southerners, as well as Southern chefs. Turner Catledge, writing for *The New York Times*, pointed out that Ulysses S. Grant had developed an appreciation for grits in the 1860s. It has also been rumored that the Florida-based owner of Dixie Lily grits, Cecil Webb, shipped a weekly box of grits to the White House during Dwight D. Eisenhower's eight-year term. (Although it's not clear whether Eisenhower received them, or ate them.) And through Lyndon B. Johnson's presidential library, we know that LBJ's favorite foods included a dish of deer sausage, scrambled eggs, and grits.

Outside the White House walls, grits have also been known for their ability to make or break a presidential candidate. Carter's genuine love of grits added to his appeal and authenticity—his democratic approach to life—especially with the working class. But others could immediately be pinned for pandering when evoking the comforting Southern dish with what seemed like insincerity. During the 2012 campaign cycle, Michigan-born Mitt Romney learned this the hard way. He was on a campaign swing through Jackson, Mississippi, when he greeted a crowd with a lilting, "Morning, y'all" and then professed his enjoyment of "cheesy grits, y'all." The crowd cheered enthusiastically—but the entire moment, which was captured and continually reviewed by the twenty-four-hour television news cycle, immediately took on a more colorful layer. Not only had the "y'all" been forced, as commentators pointed out, but his naming of the dish was incorrect. As writer John Birdsall noted in an article that ran on Chow.com a short time later, grits prepared with cheese are simply called "'cheese grits.' Always."

Newt Gingrich, who was on the same trail as Romney at the time, followed up on the episode when he arrived at a restaurant in Mobile, Alabama, for a breakfast meeting, during which he responded to his rival's misstep, announcing that he himself ate grits regularly. "I just want to reassure all of you that I have had some acquaintance in a variety of forms, whether it's with shrimp, with cheese, with gravy, whatever," he pledged. He understood grits, he continued. And he believed it was "politically important" to do so.

Grits are not the only food that has cost a candidate their political footing, of course. It's just one of many dishes that seem to get bungled by visiting politicians as they tirelessly traipse across the US in search of votes and donation dollars. A tamale, eaten with the corn husk wrapper still intact, haunted Gerald Ford. Broccoli was denounced by George H. W. Bush. The word *potato* tripped up Dan Quayle during a spelling bee. And arugula helped shape the perception of Barack Obama as an elitist.

Eventually, grits did help Obama, though, since in his hands (and mouth), the dish conjured authenticity. A black man eating an everyman's breakfast dish left a notable impression. So, on the campaign trail, he ordered them at nearly every stop. This wasn't necessarily a political move—Obama really does like grits, as evidenced by his regular, pre-presidential visits to Valois, a cafeteria-style restaurant in Chicago, where the restaurant reinforced his regularity by hanging a red, white, and blue themed menu of "President Obama's Favorites" on the wall. The list included three types of omelets—steak, Mediterranean, and a veggie-filled, egg-white one—as well as a dish of two eggs with bacon or sausage, all with the option of grits on the side.

In the right hands, grits can be a strong political ally. In the case of those Southern schools and their fight against the whole-grain aggression, grits did, eventually, get their due. In May 2017, after the nutrition director's visit to Congress, Trump's secretary of agriculture, Sonny Perdue, shifted the timelines on the Obama-era requirements, allowing schools to take up waivers protecting them from the regulation that "all grains on the lunch line must be rich in whole grains." It was a small victory for the supporters of grits in schools—but one that still had rippling repercussions.

The announcement came within the same ruling that said sodium reductions, which would have gone into effect with the Healthy, Hunger-Free Kids Act, would not be required in school lunches. The act would have brought sodium levels down from 1,230 milligrams per student per day to 935 milligrams, but the restrictions were pulled back, meaning that those who were fighting for more relaxed regulations now had two major wins—and both, it could be argued, scored big points for flavor.

But those victories came at the cost of nutrition. Many of the schools that fought for the whole-grain restriction pullback were located in some of the poorest and most nutritionally deficient Southern districts, and their nutrition directors, who valiantly took up the fight to keep partial-grain (and likely industrially produced) grits on their lunchroom lines also managed to keep sodium at startlingly high levels—even as some Southern states continually report the highest levels of obesity in the country. A gross misuse of grits as a political tool? Perhaps. But at least the students of the Alabama school system are now able to stomach their grits.

Field Politics

If, as agricultural activist and author Wendell Berry says, "Eating is an agricultural act," then, author Michael Pollan surmised, it's also a political one. So, too, is cooking. To think about, produce, cook with, and eat corn in the form of grits in this country today is to engage in a political act—knowingly or not.

In the massive and increasingly resource-draining industrial agriculture system, corn is one of the most politically polarizing crops. A monoculture that eats up valuable natural resources, it is now being grown in the US at a rate of more than 15 billion bushels per year, with about 205 million of those bushels going toward the production of cereal.

The reason for corn's growth as a commodity mostly centers around its increasing profitability. The yield per acre of corn has nearly doubled, thanks to the introduction of genetically modified corn, which the US approved in 1995.[14] There's also been an increasing demand for ethanol, derived from corn oil, meaning farmers have constant demand.

Because of this, corn has become, in many places, a mono-culture. Not only does this system lock farmers into the ebbs and flows of a singular crop market, but, more terrifyingly, it depletes natural resources. Monocultures require the use of more water, more pesticides, and more fossil fuels. Nutrients are never added back to the soil naturally, which undermines the health of the top-soil. It also pushes out crop diversity—wheat, soybeans, sugar beets, barley, and sunflowers have all but disappeared from acres of the Midwest as farmers find a seemingly endless rise in profits as they raise more corn.

Meanwhile, that same corn ends up in millions of boxes of grits each year. Corn fuels the cereal-production industry, which further contributes to the industrial agriculture cycle. And though this might enrage those who want to see our environment spared, consider the end result for an average, working-class family: For just $1.99, a 24-ounce cylindrical cardboard container of grits might yield seventeen or more servings.

It's a frustrating back and forth that seems impossible to re-solve. But that frustration has led many in the food world to turn back to a more sustainable system, on plots both large and small, and do their part to reintroduce crop rotation, explore heirloom varieties, and work the land in the way our forefa-thers did.

Glenn Roberts, motivated originally by his interest in redis-covering and reintroducing flavor, quickly took on the political charge—since its start, his small (by comparison) production mill-ing operation has steadily and quietly waged culinary aggression against Big Agriculture. Though it's not a message he touts loudly, the very existence of Anson Mills is a form of resistance. By reintroducing heirloom varieties into commercial production, he offers chefs and consumers a small-scale weapon: the option to step far outside the frustrations that come from supporting the ongoing cycle of damage Big Ag creates.

During my time at the Anson Mills facility, as Glenn walked me through the milling rooms and showed me squirreled-away bags full of "critical reserve" heirloom seeds, I saw that behind the curtain, under the film of flour, hidden among all those bins, there was magic in the ancient varieties of grains he insisted on carrying forth. And each seed held not only the preservation of history but also the powerful weapon of small, slow food. Each grain, passed along via seed, was being grown by the hands of small-plot farmers around the country, all of whom Glenn had vetted based on their location, farming practices, and commitment to the conscientious stewardship of their small corners of the earth. Each field, each farmer, Glenn said, was a little point of flickering light.

And then, in the milling process, I could see the other end of this new, old-school supply chain. Set in the heart of a small, working-class Southern city, Anson's production facility was pumping out dozens of varieties of heirloom grains into easily consumable, flavor-packed products. Walking through the surprisingly small and purposefully unkempt operation—practically a not-for-profit, according to its founder—was like witnessing the Little Engine that Could, chugging "I think I can, I think I can" as it pushes ever upward in the fight against the industrial food system.

Eventually, we were back in Glenn's office, where he pulled out an unmarked bottle of hooch. He wanted me to taste for myself, in raw, liquid form, the results that his efforts could yield. The white-lightning whiskey was young, almost green, but had a smooth fatness at the center. The sharp edges, I could tell, would eventually flatten out with plenty of time in a charred oak barrel. Though it was a liquid, what we tasted out of the bottle was just another version of grits.

Putting the bottle down, Glenn eyed me. "What's your two-sentence elevator pitch on Jimmy Red?" he asked. What I knew was that Jimmy Red was an heirloom variety of corn that had gotten a ton of media attention ever since a South Carolina grower recovered several cobs of it and started repatriating it in a small field near the coast. It also stood, I soon realized, as a beacon in the ever-strengthening fight against Big Ag.

"Ted Chewning," he stated. "You're going to want to know about different colors of grits, and you're going to want to know about Jimmy Red. So you have to talk to Ted."

The first time I heard about, and tasted, Jimmy Red grits was at Husk Nashville in the fall of 2015. It was the main component of the Plate of Southern Vegetables, which had led me to my conversation with Sean Brock about the storytelling device of vegetables. The grits inside the cone-shaped dish the server placed before me, he mentioned casually, were Jimmy Red grits from Geechie Boy in South Carolina. I mentally took note of the name before dipping my spoon in. The bite was luscious and sang with corn flavor. These were perfectly cooked grits, meaning they were creamy but with heft, and bite after flavor-packed bite, they tasted as though they had been bathed in ocean water and herbal tea.

The story of Jimmy Red—its discovery and resurrection—had spread quickly into and across the culinary communities of South Carolina and beyond. Thanks to servers like the one at Husk, who were casually name-dropping the product and its miller tableside, as well as the many food writers who were chasing down its origins, the corn was climbing into the consciousness of food lovers all over the country. For a year or two, it seemed, food writers across the South and beyond were going bananas for this heirloom corn.

For a full picture of Jimmy Red—where it came from, how and where it was being grown, and why it was suddenly a darling of the Lowcountry culinary world—I turned, as Glenn had suggested, to Ted Chewning. A kind-eyed, soft-spoken farmer in his early seventies, Ted had spent most of his life farming organically on a plot of land on John's Island, South Carolina. He'd once held a day job in marketing, but farming was Ted's passion. He raised pigs for sausage, letting the animals roam and forage on forested lands, and also planted several acres of organic vegetables, both for his own use and to sell at farmers' markets. For a time, Ted ran the Colleton County farmers' market, but retired a few years back so he could focus on the one hundred acres he and his wife had purchased in Colleton, where he still grows vegetables for his own use. (He also still raises animals and produces sausage, but it's a much smaller operation these days.)

Ted's passion project was seed saving—and that was what he was most eager to talk about on the muggy July morning I visited his farm. As I approached Ted's property on Augusta Highway, I noticed that a few other farms nearby were growing corn—the yellowing stalks reached high into the summer sky. Pulling past the Sweet Bay Acres sign and down a tree-lined stretch of dirt, I found Ted himself, standing in front of his cottage-like house. "You found me," he said, smiling and shaking my hand firmly.

We walked toward a two-acre plot where a permanent greenhouse structure ran down the length of a growing row. The plot was filled with a variety of vegetables and fruit trees, which worked together to create their own ecosystem. To one side, a small roped-off field held about a dozen rows of corn—green and golden stalks that stretched well over nine feet high, much taller than the yellowing stalks I'd seen on my way in.

"That's the Jimmy Red," Ted said, walking me toward the plot. Standing tall off the stalks, each ear seemed almost fully mature, packed with kernels. Ted carefully ripped one down, turning it upward to show me a tuft of bloodred tassels. The husk of the corn was the golden yellow of seasoned hay, but, as he pulled away the drying layers, rows of shimmery-red, gem-like kernels peeked out. Jimmy Red was a work of art.

"Some of this is sketchy history. But we've been able to document some of it—so I guess it's mostly true," Ted said, smiling. The corn had come to him from a friend who owned a feed-and-seed store nearby. These cobs, apparently, were part of a crop that another man had planted just before he died. That grower hadn't lived long enough to harvest the crop, and Ted's friend had found the ears of corn growing in the man's field. The harvest was shot, but his friend had managed to collect just a couple of intact ears and gifted them to Ted.

With little more than the planter's name and an obituary, Ted researched the grower's history and traced him back to his birth date and place: 1895, Screven County, Georgia. The man's moves weren't well documented, but eventually, Ted learned, he wound up farming in Colleton County.

Ted had received the cobs about fifteen years back, and planted the seed on his isolated property—the location was right because it was several hundred yards away from any other cornfields, meaning the open-pollinated variety wouldn't cross with another breed. He was still careful to plant either before or after others in the area were planting to ensure his crop wouldn't be pollinating at the same time theirs were. The first crop—seed he'd pulled from about two ears of corn—yielded several rows. From that, Ted pulled more seed, preserving what he could. Slowly, year after year, Ted planted the Jimmy Red, rotating fields or taking a season off here and there depending on what else was growing. He grew the corn out and pulled seeds from each crop, freezing it until the following season, all in an effort to create a pure source of seed. Once he had a solid supply, he started passing handfuls along to others, including Glenn at Anson Mills.

Glenn, forever researching heirloom varieties, sent the corn to a researcher to have it genetically tested. Ted also gifted seed to Dr. Brian Ward, a research scientist at Clemson University's Coastal Research and Education Center (CREC), as well as Sean Brock of Husk, and Greg Johnsman of Geechie Boy. Brian planted the seed for research and preservation. Sean planted the corn in his own garden in Charleston. And Greg, who was just getting himself into the milling game at the time, started growing it out on his wife's family's land on Edisto Island.

Through Glenn's research, it was determined that this corn did not have the same genetic characteristics of Bloody Butcher, another bright red heirloom variety. It had a few blue corn traits and produced an almost purplish-red product when ground into grits and mixed with hot water. This corn was a hardy species, resistant to insect damage, particularly the European earworm and weevils that dogged corn crops in this part of South Carolina. There also tended to be fewer seeds per cob, and it wasn't a high-yielding producer, so where a hybrid variety of corn might offer up 150 bushels per acre, Jimmy Red would only yield about 100—meaning it was a complicated variety to get right from year to year.

Growing the corn was one project. Figuring out what to do with it became another. First, it needed a name. Without much written history about the variety, Ted and Glenn had to think through its possible uses over time. The corn, they surmised, had likely been grown for moonshining. And, during that time in history—the early to mid-1900s—it might have been grown out on James Island, an area that for many years was used strictly for agriculture. Glenn chose the name arbitrarily: "Jimmy Red," for James Island and the corn's color.

As Ted relayed the tale, my mind wandered back to the moment when settlers bestowed a name on an unfamiliar dish of steaming cooked-down corn: grits. Like that dish, this variety of corn was one that had likely been grown and passed along through the hands of indigenous women. Perhaps it was originally crossed and bred a thousand years ago, and grown in this stretch of the world for generations before this man from Screven County started growing it himself. And now here we were, holding a cob of corn that two old grain buffs, in cementing their own version of the story, had given a name. With that, Ted and Glenn had become the carriers of the tale. Once again, I wondered about

those original cultivators and where their stories had trailed off—
and, with this development of rediscovery, whether they would
ever come to light.

Both Ted and Glenn began playing with the crop in different
ways. Milling was the natural process—this being dent corn, it
was traditionally good for two things: whiskey and grits. Ted used
a friend's mill to crack his grains; Greg Johnsman, who had a
vast collection of antique milling equipment, started milling the
corn on his own equipment. And Glenn milled it, too, using
his cold-chilling process to help preserve the flavor of the grits.

But all who came across the seed, it seemed, saw the corn's
potential beyond grits. Glenn introduced it to a man named Scott
Blackwell around 2013, who, at the time, was trying to get a new
distillery off the ground in Charleston. Called High Wire Distilling, the brand's focus was to create spirits out of uniquely Southern
crops, such as a whiskey made from sorghum. Glenn brought
Scott to the CREC, where the miller showed the distiller a table
full of corn varieties that might be good for making whiskey.

"Which is the best?" Scott asked.

"This one," Glenn said, holding up a cob of Jimmy Red.

❋

Ted walked me inside his farmhouse, where a wood stove sat to
one side and a weaving loom, looking as though it had been used
recently, sat near a window. The space opened up toward a
kitchen with a large island at its center. Atop the wood counter,
Ted had set out a few bottles of whiskey. Two were made by High
Wire, both with Jimmy Red corn. There was also a bottle of malt
liquor hidden in a brown paper bag—a collaboration between

Charleston's Revelry Brewing Co. and Sean Brock, it was called Amber Waves and had been brewed with a few varieties of heritage grains, including Jimmy Red.

Ted picked up one of the whiskeys, a ceramic red-and-black bottle—the bottle itself had been a special collaboration between High Wire and Le Creuset, the high-end cookware company. He pointed to the wax seal, which was still intact. "I'll open this one for the birth of my first grandchild," he said with a smile. "That's my pride and joy in there. I saved those seeds from extinction."

Curious about what all had gone into the making of Ted's prized bottle, I took a drive into Charleston for a visit with Scott Blackwell and Ann Marshall, the couple behind High Wire. Scott, a pastry chef by trade, had started his career in Greenville, South Carolina, where he owned a baking and packaging company. He'd gotten excited about craft beers in the early 1990s and started brewing his own—he thought he'd sell the bakery eventually and open a brewery. By the time the bakery sold, though, the craft beer market had exploded. He and Ann did some market research and decided to switch gears—they would turn their attention to liquor instead.

Scott wasn't a distiller—he hardly drank liquor at all, in fact. But as part of the couple's market research, he started tasting the vast variety of booze being pumped out into the world and realized that gin could taste like pine needles and that bourbon could have layers of flavor. His goal, he decided, would be to create a distillery that told a story around its products.

It was Southern Foodways Alliance director John T. Edge who gave Scott the idea of making something out of sorghum. The two were walking through Charleston's Marion Square and Scott had just eaten a sticky sorghum cake at the restaurant Fig. "What about sorghum whiskey?" John T. asked. "Could you try something like that?"

Scott had worked with sorghum as a sugar alternative at his bakery but hadn't considered working it into liquor. With John T. as his muse, Scott soon found his niche.

Eventually, Scott connected with Glenn at CREC and, through the Center, came to know Ted. At the time, Ted was still the keeper of the Jimmy Red seed and held a tight rein on who was getting what. But after meeting Scott, he liked the idea of seeing the corn turned into a whiskey. Because Scott didn't have any land or a mill, he utilized the resources at CREC and Ted's seed to grow out a production crop and relied on Glenn to do his milling. The first season, 2014, he was out in the field while they planted, with Brian Ward, Glenn, and Ted all contributing their expertise along the way. It was a wet and rainy season, but eventually, the moisture levels on the corn were low enough that the crop could be harvested. Scott and a team of volunteers went out and broke off the stalks by hand, harvesting about two acres of Jimmy Red—some of the crop would be held for seed; the rest would go toward whiskey production.

Glenn took the corn up to Anson Mills to have it cleaned and cold-milled, but insisted that the milling occur on the same day that it would be put into the mash bill, or the mix of grains that would be cooked and fermented to start the whiskey-making process. The crop came down in batches, with Glenn milling it and sending it down to Charleston on the days when the Blackwells could start the mash immediately.

"We had mashed enough white corn by that point that we

knew what the general flavor should be. But the Jimmy Red, we noticed, had a different kind of sweetness. It was like the difference between sugar and honey—it had an earthy flavor," Scott said. The Jimmy Red mash also produced a thick oily cap once it went into the fermenter. "We'd never seen that on yellow or white corn. It smelled like a mix between peanut butter and Laffy Taffy." Scott laughed. They ended up pumping the oily cap over and into the mixture before distilling it, and when the product was finally distilled, they could feel that the oily droplets were still present. "It made it silky to the touch. When you tasted it at 120 proof, it didn't burn like other whiskeys because all of that oil would coat your tongue. It was so different than any other whiskey we'd ever tried."

Scott walked me into the distillery, where they were in the middle of mashing a batch of Jimmy Red. I stepped gingerly up a narrow ladder toward the top of the fermentation tank. Sticking my head into the tank's tiny porthole, I breathed in deeply, inhaling the scent of steamy, malty breakfast cereal. Hot grits.

It was with my head stuck down into the mash bill that I realized how closely the miller and the distiller worked in tandem, and how the relationship between grits and whiskey had evolved. The mash bill itself was basically grits: water and ground corn combined and cooked down. The difference, Scott noted, was the grind itself. Whereas a grits miller might sift out the pericarp and separate the grits from the meal and the flour, a distiller would combine and use all those parts.

"We throw everything in because if it's got carbohydrates in it, it will turn into alcohol. That's all we care about," Scott said.

That fine line between the grits miller and the distiller had long been blurred, over and again, into one long, woven story of similar purpose. The two end products, one solid, one liquid, might differ in terms of texture, style, and, of course, resulting fortitude once consumed, but their coexistence creates a through-line for grits and whiskey, both of which are claimed as deeply Southern totems. Grits are the happy, soul-sustaining by-product of a moonshiner's bounty. Whether all moonshiners eat grits needn't matter. It's the comingling of the two, and the mythology around them both, that makes for such a captivating tale and, once again, helps thread together a story line that pits the small-batch artisan producer—whether their product be moonshine or grits—against the big industrial giants of the day.

Before Scott distilled any variety of corn, he usually gave it a taste test by milling the corn into fine grits and mixing them with boiling water for about ten minutes. The water would just barely release the flavor of the corn, not quite cooking it, but rather loosing its essence. With white varieties, he might get a blandness up front, followed by a nutty finish. Yellow kernels would bomb the palate with sweetness first, then dissipate quickly. But the Jimmy Red? After only ten minutes in water, he said, it tasted like nothing—bland. "Now, if I were to cook it down with water for a few hours, it might start to release something, which is why it could be good for grits. Especially once you add some butter." He smiled.

It's what happened to the corn during the rest of the process that made it so ideal for distilling, Scott explained. While most of the bourbon makers in Kentucky run a sour mash bill—adding a small amount of already fermented mash (hence the word *sour*) to new batches—Scott preferred a sweet mash bill, which meant he made a fresh mash each time. He was also producing the

Jimmy Red bourbon with 100 percent corn, adding no other grains to the mash.

When Julian P. Van Winkle III, president of the Old Rip Van Winkle Distillery and purveyor of his family's line of cult-followed, highly coveted Pappy Van Winkle bourbon, tasted Scott's Jimmy Red bourbon, he didn't believe it was made with only corn. He had Scott send a few samples of both the plain, unaged white spirit and the aged bourbon to him in Kentucky—and slyly took it over to the Buffalo Trace facility to have it tested. "I think you're onto something here," the patriarch said to Scott, before offering to pay any amount necessary for a bottle of the stuff. (Wisely, Ann Marshall suggested they make a trade for a bottle of Pappy instead.)

I asked Scott if he believed in Glenn's and Ted's theory that Jimmy Red had traditionally been grown as a moonshiner's corn. "It flies." He nodded. "Back in the day, when you read about the history of stills, it was mostly farmers who had stills—it was illegal, even though they weren't doing it to make money. They would just grow the stuff and they'd be curious, like 'What would that taste like as a liquor?'" I thought back to Ted's liquor stash in his kitchen and remembered spotting a large object, draped with a cloth, sitting off to the side. I'd caught the gleam of copper under the drape, but left the topic alone. Likely, I thought, if Ted did have a still, it was for the experimental purposes of a farmer.

At last, Scott and I got through with the tour and headed toward the distillery's tasting room. He pulled out a few glasses and reached far back onto one of the shelves to pull out a bottle that held a last few ounces of Jimmy Red bourbon. He opened it and held it under my nose, letting the aroma waft out. I smelled the raisin-y sweet scent of a well-aged liquor.

"That's two years old," he said, and smiled before pouring me a splash. I inhaled the scent deeply and swirled it in my glass before taking a small sip. I expected heat and the lip-pulsing tingle of a young bourbon. What I got was pure, silky sweetness, a satin cloth against my tongue, and sugar that nearly knocked me back. There was the flavor of raw corn underneath and around the sweetness, but at the center, it was all bright, earthy syrup, and tasted as though it had been sitting in a barrel for a decade.

At the time of our meeting, Scott was deep into an important experiment with Jimmy Red. At one point, he pulled out a series of charts, graphs, and statistics that a lab had provided for him. He had worked with four different farmers to grow out the Jimmy Red seed at four different locations around South Carolina. Different soils, row distances, irrigation systems, harvesting methods—each had their own practices, and Scott was trying to see what would happen to each crop once it was distilled. He created one liquor from each batch of corn, then sent samples of the pure unaged liquor to a geneticist, who measured a range of differences between the final products. From the measurements of proteins, oils, fibers, and the spirit itself, the results showed where certain harvests were going to take the final product.

They also showed genetic differences in the corn itself, proving that, as purely as various growers have tried to preserve the original Jimmy Red, each was growing seeds with a different set of characteristics. Which was the original Jimmy Red? It almost didn't matter, Scott admitted. What did matter was that there was one grower who could produce the same exact corn, time and time again, which would allow Scott to produce a consistent bourbon with each harvest.

Essentially, Scott was conducting a data-driven analysis of the corn's *terroir*. By distilling the four growers' corn individually—making four different bourbons from the same corn grown in four different ways—he was providing a fairly rigorous study of *terroir*. Each bourbon, especially when tested in their raw, unaged state, showcased the flavors of the place where the corn was grown—one might be sweeter, one might be earthier, and one might exude nuttiness, all because of the soil quality, climate conditions, and growing methods used. My mind raced back to Sean Brock's comment about *terroir*, and I saw that Scott was already two steps ahead. If bourbon could act differently with each crop of corn, so, too, could a plate of grits.

That first batch of High Wire Jimmy Red bourbon, pulled from the 2014 harvest of two acres from the CREC fields, yielded about two barrels of liquid gold. Scott let those age for two years, finally bottling the product in fall 2016. There were just over two hundred bottles from that first run, one of which was sitting on Ted Chewning's kitchen counter. The Blackwells generated some buzz before releasing the bourbon to the public, and the day it went on sale, they sold out of every bottle in eleven minutes. It was a victory for a small, Southern, artisanal producer—but also a win for the corn itself. With the demand firmly in place, production crops of that finicky, hard-to-protect Jimmy Red corn were all but guaranteed.

✳

While the Blackwells put Jimmy Red to work in the bottle, Greg and Betsy Johnsman at Geechie Boy put the heirloom corn to work via mill. As both grower and miller, Greg had control over the entire product, from seed to harvest to mill to bag. His expertise was put to use both in the field, growing the corn, and in the milling process, where his application of old, low-heat-generating antique milling machinery coaxed the flavor out from those precious heirloom grains. Greg's battle was the fight of the small, family-owned farm and business—and it was being fought in both the field and the millroom.

Greg planted his first major production crop of Jimmy Red, started from seed he received from Ted Chewning, in 2013—but because of where he planted it and his timing, the entire crop was exposed to another variety of corn through cross-pollination. The same thing happened in 2014. By 2015, he'd figured out the system, and most of the crop came to harvest. Then they lost about a third of the corn to bad rains, but what they salvaged was pure, as far as Greg could tell. They harvested, dried, and stored what little of the crop they could get, saving some of it for seed, and milled a little bit of it that fall as their first production run of Jimmy Red grits. It was a huge load of work for what resulted in just a few bags of grits—but the efforts were worthwhile in that it carried the grain just a few inches further toward preservation. The grits, which they sold in two-pound bags for twelve dollars apiece, appeared speckled, a mix of the kernels' red exterior with the creamy white particulates of the interior.

Greg started growing other heirloom varieties, too, some of which he milled into grits, others of which became purely experimental or were grown in an effort to revive the grain, such as an heirloom rye, which he milled and sold to bakeries, as well as a Guinea Flint corn and a blue corn variety.

Greg's dual role as both a small, family farmer and an artisan producer meant he was constantly switching hats. When he wasn't in the field, caring for his heirloom varieties, monitoring moisture, or better understanding how certain crops were faring, he was on the road, peddling his grits to chefs and retailers. Recently, he'd partnered with a restaurateur to open a breakfast-and-lunch spot in the heart of Charleston called Miller's All Day, where he placed an antique mill in the front window to show people how the machines worked.

The forces working against Greg were plentiful. The Low-country is not really ideal for grain milling, mostly due to the humidity. Because of that, he was constantly working on ways to dehumidify his corn—using certain variables both in the field and after the harvest to "play God" with his crops.

For an article that ran in *The New York Times* in 2011, Greg and Sean Brock used liquid nitrogen to chill a batch of corn down super fast before milling it to make cornmeal. They were trying to determine whether flash-freezing the corn changed the flavor, which was a theory Greg had developed based on anecdotal evidence. He'd heard that historically, farmers in his region would go to the community mills at sunrise before the heat of the day affected the machines. This helped preserve the flavor of the corn and kept the machines running smoothly.

Their experiment mimicked what Glenn Roberts was doing at Anson Mills—and it worked. Greg proved that he could instill flavor by keeping the temperature low from storage to the point of milling. But Greg wasn't going to be able to install the same cold-milling techniques Glenn used regularly. Instead, he relied on his collection of antique machines—they couldn't run fast enough or generate enough heat to overtly change the flavor of the corn and, in the end, they provided the right coarseness and quality for what Greg was looking to sell.

Bigger than any other battle—against market forces, competition, or governmental checks—was Greg's struggle to wrangle Mother Nature. In early fall 2016, he harvested his entire crop of Jimmy Red corn in mid-August, weeks before he normally might. They'd planted early, and even though harvesting that early in August meant the moisture content in the corn was high and consequently they'd face issues drying the crop, it was better to do it then than risk a hurricane wiping out the entire crop later—which, if they had let it sit, is exactly what would have happened when Hurricane Matthew swung through a few weeks later.

Months after Matthew's storm waters flooded Greg's fields, the family faced a reckoning. Adair had lost an entire fall crop of commercial tomatoes. The fields were devastated. After forty-five years in the tomato business, Adair was forced to shut down his operation. It wasn't just the storm—it had been three bad years in a row for the tomato crops, and the losses were too much to recover from.

Since then, Greg and his family have turned their attention toward rice. Greg has planted a few fields of Charleston Gold Rice since the storm, and he's brought his father-in-law and a few other family members in on the project as well. There's no guarantee that this new grain will prosper, but at least the transition will keep the agricultural work of the farm moving forward.

As a farmer, seedsman, and preservationist, Greg's work is an ongoing march. Like Jennifer Nicely and her family's struggle to find a market for their products, Greg's work requires pricing his goods in such a way that he can make a living and pay the people around him for their work, too. Because nothing really matters if the family can't make a living off their land.

Yes, Geechie Boy grits have gotten glowing reviews and are served and mentioned by name at high-end restaurants. And yes, growing Jimmy Red corn and other revived grain varieties has given Geechie Boy a chance to appear in some of the most celebrated kitchens in the country. But does any of that matter if the grains won't grow? Just because a small family of farmers works with intensity every day doesn't guarantee success. It's a plight that all small farmers face. But Greg, who wages his battle daily in the fields or working his antique machines, keeps pushing the ball forward, offering another small-scale alternative to the industrial food system—and, more important, ensuring that his family business will survive.

✳

The efforts being made by Greg, Glenn, Ted, and Sean Brock to hold on to and protect certain varieties of seed are not new. The acts of seed saving and grain revival have been used for centuries, and typically have been female driven. Today, there's a renewed interest in seed saving as its been given more and more mainstream attention—and for those who have been doing it for a lifetime, that discussion is a welcome introduction.

John Coykendall, master gardener at Blackberry Farm, works a small plot of land that sits just over a knoll, past the luxury Tennessee property's huge red dining barn. Inside a gardening house, a quaint yet luxurious little cottage with a tin roof and faded red wooden walls, John makes his office. A sliding barn door opens into a cool, dim room. Climbing vines make their way up one of the walls, bathing half the building in green. Out front, two robin's-egg blue rocking chairs sit facing the garden. Like something plucked from the Shire of Tolkien, it is a vision of rustic simplicity—an Instagrammable paradise.

John is seventysomething, with bushy gray eyebrows and a soft face that bunches up in wrinkles around his bright blue eyes. In denim overalls and a blue gingham shirt, he is the very picture of the old-time Southern farmer. He grew up in Knoxville and got into seed saving at an early age, around sixteen, when he discovered a copy of the William Henry Maule Seed Catalog in an abandoned train station in Knoxville. It was filled with old varieties of vegetable seeds and, even better, colorful engraved illustrations of the plants the seeds produced.

His eye was drawn to a Tennessee sweet potato pumpkin—he liked that it was bell-shaped and white with green stripes. "Real pretty thing," he recalls. He ordered four different seeds from four different sources and kept the seeds under his pillow for the long months of winter until he could plant them. His love for old seeds snowballed from there.

John saw the catalog as a gateway into a new world of "old" plant varieties. He would ask others where to find these mysterious-looking vegetables and fruits, but rarely had luck. The Seed Savers Exchange, which is now a vast network that allows people to share and trade seeds as an effort to preserve heirloom varieties, wasn't started until 1975—before that, it was simply a hand-passing tradition, rarely recorded.

In the years before the Exchange existed, John found help through farm bulletins, where farmers would list seed for sale. His interest and ability to grow out varieties carried on throughout his life, until he arrived at Blackberry Farm about twenty years back.

John grew up eating grits. His were usually made from a stone-ground white corn, but he wouldn't turn up his nose at yellow grits, either. Born in 1943, John knew a time when there were still small local mills to be found. His family might take their corn to be ground when they needed it, or buy it from the corncrib that sat near the mill. The miller would set the stone based on whether a family wanted meal or grits.

In John's garden office on the Blackberry Farm property, broad wooden bowls are set about, as are small piles of seeds and scraps of paper scrawled with names. Freckled black-and-red beans sit under a card labeled "butterbeans" while another pile is listed as "Okra: Parkins Mammoth, Long Grain, 1913." The space smells sweet, the heavy scent of flowers and herbs mingling with sawdust. The intense colors of the beans and seeds beckon one to sift their fingers through, feeling the smooth, rounded edges and hewn bottom of each singular kernel.

John knows the stories behind each. Like many in the region, John sees seed saving for what it once was: a necessity. At one time, much of the area's population couldn't afford to purchase seeds. Every holler has had its unique varieties.

There was Bloody Butcher, which dates to 1848. It's now widely available through seed stocks, but John also has a selection that has only ever been preserved and passed along by local families. One shoe peg variety—named for its shape, which resembles an old wooden shoe peg—that was once common in Mississippi and Louisiana was named by the family who raised and preserved it. Webb Watson came to be called that because of who had held the seed last: a man named Squire Watson, who lived nearby on Big Flat Creek. The corn had actually been originated by someone named Mr. Webb and then, in 1890, Mr. Watson improved on it, so it became Webb Watson—and today, it's nearly extinct. There's Hickory King (also known in some parts as Hickory Cane), introduced in 1886 as a milling corn. In another seed catalog printed in 1888, which John has lying about, the text says "it's destined to become a favorite in the Southland," which it has. Commonly, that variety was used to make hominy, with its growers soaking it in lye water to bust off the hull and then drying it before milling it into grits.

John is not just a gardener, but someone who peers into the windows of history through his seeds. By collecting these stories, which he frequently delivers to the Seed Savers Exchange, and shares with the inn's well-paying guests, he is preserving the history of the region itself.

He's also tending one of the area's most diverse and historical kitchen gardens. For nearly twenty years, he's carefully curated a broad selection of varieties, experimenting with different seeds and crops year after year, working and reworking the land as it might have been worked before the time of tractors, when the land was tended by the hands of a small family. His agenda is more than just protecting the diversity of seeds. He is chasing flavor. Like Glenn, he wants to teach people what real food tastes like.

Being located where he is, on the edge of Appalachia, John has access to one of the country's most diverse food regions. Small plots, making up three-, five-, or ten-acre farms, once proliferated there. Just like the Sea Islands and their ability to cloak and protect the Gullah Geechee, the isolation of Appalachia's hilly terrain protects diversity, and in some cases increases it. For open-pollinated corn varieties, especially, the distance and landscape between growing patches has long been significant—it means that seed strains can (and have) remained pure and intact for generations, seeing modification only when the seed is selected or moved somewhere else. Seeds have long been traded over hills, intentionally moved by people, but otherwise, the corn varieties have remained protected.

Today, John maintains the tradition of milling his own grits with a faded old red hand-crank mill that's attached to a wooden tabletop. Spinning the handle with one arm, he uses the other to pour a handful of Bloody Butcher kernels into the mill. The grinding mechanism, which is metal instead of stone, has grates that shift over one another to grind the corn. John puts his whole body into it, getting the mill up to speed. After the corn has gone through once, he pours the ground bits back into the feeder to create a finer grind. He does this three or four more times, creating a light cornmeal. He stops when he is satisfied, working at it for ten minutes for a small batch to share with a friend, or for much longer, and likely with more help, when he's grinding enough for, say, 150 servings that might arrive on the plate at one of Blackberry Farm's celebrated restaurants.

John uses his role at Blackberry and his space on the property to carry on local traditions, but in his own way, he also uses it as a platform to send a louder message. His is a fight for regional cuisine, and for the preservation of old foodways. By saving these seeds and continuing the growing traditions of the area, he is a living museum of knowledge—one that may not be accessible to most but is a treasure trove nonetheless. The resort, which can charge a mortgage payment for some of its rooms, has invested heavily into John's work, and passes it along by hiring a small army of apprentices each year, who come to the property to work the land alongside John. As he passes his knowledge down to them, they, too, will work to preserve and carry forth the traditions of Appalachian agriculture.

๛

HICKORY KING GRITS WITH PRESERVED GARDEN VEGETABLES

Courtesy of Cassidee Dabney, Executive Chef, The Barn at Blackberry Farm

Serves 4 as a side dish

"I love taking vegetables grown in the summer garden at Blackberry Farm and preserving them for use outside their growing season. Adding that summer sweetness and brightness to a dish is an opportunity to showcase seasonal flavor any time of year. It creates a taste of remembering the past as well as a hopefulness looking toward the future. This is my go-to grits recipe, perfect for enjoying in any season. We grow a few varieties of corn on Blackberry Farm, but Hickory King is our favorite. It mills easily and retains a subtle sweetness after cooking."

Pickled Sweet Peppers

2 cups sliced sweet peppers

½ cup white balsamic vinegar

½ cup water

½ cup sugar

Grits

2 cups water

2 cups milk

Salt

1 cup grits

Butter

To Serve

Preserved Garden Eggplant (recipe follows)

Fennel pollen

Crispy fried hominy

MAKE THE PICKLED SWEET PEPPERS: Put the peppers in a large bowl. In a small saucepan, combine the vinegar, water, and sugar and bring to a boil. Pour the hot liquid over the peppers and let cool to room temperature. Cover and refrigerate for up to 3 weeks.

MAKE THE GRITS: In a medium saucepan, combine the water, milk, and salt to taste and bring to a boil. Slowly whisk in the grits, and continue whisking until they begin to thicken. Reduce the heat to maintain a low simmer. Cover and cook, stirring occasionally, for 1 to 2 hours. Let the cooked grits rest at room temperature for 1 hour. Add butter, taste, and season with additional salt if desired. Reheat if necessary before serving.

TO PLATE: Spoon the finished grits into individual bowls. Top with preserved eggplant and pickled peppers that have been warmed in their juices. Sprinkle with fennel pollen and crispy fried hominy. Serve as a side dish or a vegetable course.

PRESERVED GARDEN EGGPLANT

"It seems like every summer, we have more eggplants than we know what to do with. This recipe is a great way to preserve and extend the flavors of summer into the other seasons."

DAY 1: Peel 4 eggplants, roughly chop, and toss in a bowl with excessive salt. Place on a perforated pan and set another pan on top of the eggplant. Put a small amount of weight in the top pan to help drain liquid from the eggplant. Let sit overnight.

DAY 2: In a large saucepan, combine 2 parts water and 1 part white wine vinegar and add salt. Add the drained eggplant and bring to a boil. Cook until slightly tender, then drain and place the eggplant on clean kitchen towels to dry overnight.

DAY 3: Shave a few heads of garlic into a cold pan. Add 1 tablespoon Aleppo pepper, 3 tablespoons Greek oregano, and 4 cups high-quality extra-virgin olive oil. Bring the oil to a simmer just to season the oil, then remove from the heat. Toss the eggplant with the oil. Pack the eggplant into an airtight container and pour in any remaining oil. Let rest for at least 1 week before serving.

The Miller Activists

The notion that a return to simpler traditions, like seed saving and small-batch food production, could be a political act that started many decades ago. For grits, the turning point came in the 1970s and '80s, when small community mills started making a comeback across the South. War Eagle Mill in Rogers, Arkansas, was given new life in 1973 when it was purchased by the Medlin family—the original mill had been built in 1832 but had been destroyed by flooding and fires several times. The Medlins rebuilt it, complete with an undershot waterwheel, and brought it into the modern era. There was Logan Turnpike Mill in North Georgia, bought by George and Cecilia Holland in 1986 and later moved to a new location where they still operate a 1916 Williams mill on an antique hit-and-miss engine to mill their grits, which are sourced from local corn growers. Other old mills, like Weisenberger and Falls Mills, which had been milling corn and other grains, started milling grits regularly in the 1990s. In the 2010s, new mills like Geechie Boy and Congaree came online, as did other small operations, including Colonial Milling in Pauline, South Carolina, run by first-generation farmers, and Canewater Farms in the Appalachian Mountains of North Georgia, which grows and mills organic corn. Not all these millers set out with political intentions, but they have, in their own ways, stood in resistance to the pressures of Big Agriculture.

I considered the role of the modern-day miller, specifically those who have taken up the grits torch recently, and came to understand three differing forms of motivation.

There was Steve Gantt, a historical preservationist and tinkerer who was working to ensure that old-time traditions didn't entirely disappear. There was Mark Keisler, who was moonlighting as a miller after doing his day job as a surgeon, and growing heirloom varieties of corn on about thirty acres in South Carolina. His motivation was to update and move forward the act of water-powered milling. And finally, there was Jim Barkley, a car dealer turned heirloom grits producer, whose marketing and high-cost production had positioned him for the *Southern Living* demographic, or those looking for nostalgia in their local food movement. His motivation was to create a self-sustaining small family farm that could adapt to the demands of an ever-growing market.

※

Steve Gantt plays the role of miller as preservationist with his operation Gantt's Stonemill Store. On the outskirts of Columbia, in Leesville, South Carolina, you'll find the store after driving down a broad graveled path called Swamp Rabbit Road. It's hard to spot, being that it's not much more than a small collection of cabins—a home, a small general store, and a barn that looks like it's seen better days.

Steve wears overalls and a plaid shirt, struggles a bit with his gait, and wears his glasses down low on his nose, peering to give visitors the once-over. Inside his country store he sells grits in cloth bags, country hams, and a whole lot of nostalgia.

His barn holds various pieces of machinery, including a few old hand-crank mills, one of which is at least a century old. There are axes, handmade hammers, and other metal-smithing tools hanging from the walls alongside old Pepsi ads and other rusted tin signs.

To one side, perched on a bright red wooden box, sits a tall, dust-filmed Meadows mill, built in the 1920s. Near it, close to the door, there's an old red grits separator that takes up almost an entire wall; Steve built that one himself, opting to put his own skills to use rather than pay several thousand dollars for a new one.

When the machine is running, a wheel that's attached to one side is connected to a long shaft that pumps up and down with each turn of the wheel. The sound is like a fast-moving rocking chair, the *tap-tapping* of wooden planks. The shaft causes the sifter to rock from side to side, moving the ground-up corn inside down along the tilted screen.

Steve has eight or nine other mills scattered around the property, all in various states of repair. One is just a pile of steel plates—the walls of the mill, broken down and stacked up like puzzle pieces. A lifelong tinkerer, Steve was a firefighter for thirty-five years, but also spent his lifetime studying the arts of blacksmithing, hammer making, hog killing, and history keeping. He's proud of his wood-burning stove, where he likes to make biscuits, moving the pan around just so in order to brown the bottoms in all the right spots. Every winter, he makes a handful of massive fruitcakes, using an old washtub that he's cut down to a shallow dish to bake them over live heat. A small collection of self-made tongs and hammers sits at the base of the stove, waiting for his hands to put them to work. Seemingly a man of little means, Steve is brimming with so many nearly lost skills that he's actually wealthier in natural resources than most monied men.

Walking into his general store, a space trapped in time, you pass through a creaking wooden screen door and into another era. It's not so much a retail space but a time preserve. A chest-high counter, where checkouts occur, holds countless scraps of paper, nubs of pencils, wooden bowls, and dust-covered notebooks. The shelves on one wall are lined with books that were printed more than a century ago. Old maps with barely there roads outlined on yellowing paper lean against the walls. He has a map of a town called Steadman—which no longer exists. A tornado wiped it out before they could build the infrastructure, which is sketched out on the map as proposed land plots and streets.

In a book he's writing, Steve talks about old times and old ways, like making corn fodders and cooking on a wood stove. There's one small refrigerator set up on a shelf, where Steve stores a few bags of blue, white, and yellow corn grits. As a steward and purveyor of the past, Steve hopes that just by continuing the tradition of running a country store, and acting as the local miller, he can help carry the "old ways" into the future.

❊

Dr. Mark Keisler has become a miller in order to revive the art of water-powered milling. A surgeon and ophthalmologist in Lexington, South Carolina, Mark claims to have gristmilling in his blood. Milling grits and cornmeal is his "professional hobby," one he likens to golf.

Mark and his wife, Ann, live in Gilbert, South Carolina (close to Steve Gantt, who Mark considers a friendly competitor). On their property sit a pond and several acres of pine and oak trees. The house itself is large and lovely, decorated like it belongs in a glossy home magazine. Glass doors open up to a large patio, and down a short slope, a wooden millhouse sits a short distance away.

Ann is not what you might think of when you hear "miller's wife." (She rolls her eyes at the term.) An attorney practicing family and estate planning and real estate law full-time, she is happy to be the support staff to her husband's hobby—labeling and shipping bags of grits, and updating the website with recipes.

Mark is not what you might think of when you hear "miller,"

either. Wearing a pressed white shirt, his graying white hair set neatly in place above wire-rimmed glasses, he looks every bit the part of an off-duty doctor and surgeon, one whose hands are rarely dirty.

Well-read and highly knowledgeable about corn, milling, and farming, Mark's obsession started when he began experimenting with growing different varieties of corn in varying colors, shapes, and sizes. Now, he plants varieties like a Pencil Cob corn, a Carolina Gourdseed, a Loman yellow corn, and a Floriani flint red corn, on about 30 acres scattered between this property and a few other pieces of land. Each plot is isolated so he can grow these open-pollinated heirloom breeds and make seed selections from his own lots. He has no reliance on outside seed salesmen or interference from industrial ag.

Milling was Mark's dream for years. He first started playing around with it in the 1980s, and then got down to it in earnest on this property around 2008 or 2009. The millhouse that sits behind their home, trimmed in green, looks like it might have been pulled from a Grimms' fairy tale. The construction of the mill building has been years in the making. It's Mark's passion project. The floors are made of hickory, while other parts are heart pine, and all of the wood has been culled from the property. Out to one side, a 12-foot waterwheel is attached to the building—painted a glossy fire engine red with black trim.

Inside, the parts and pieces of an old horizontal stone mill are gathered, but they're not fully intact or functioning. Mark has collected the various gears, stones, and parts and pieces from out-of-commission mills that have been dismantled or left to fall into disrepair—he's taking his time in reconstructing them into a functioning mill. A horizontal bed stone, which dates back to the 1800s, is set within a wooden base, but the top stone sits off to the side—it hasn't been dressed properly and needs to go to a stone cutter to be repaired.

While he takes his time building a water-powered mill from the ground up, he uses a 1920s motor-powered mill, which is set in a building about seven miles from his home, to mill his grits and cornmeal. When orders come in, he gets home from work, eats dinner, and scurries over to the mill room, sometimes starting up the machine at eleven p.m. or midnight so he can fill his orders.

Mark and Ann's life is full—both work full-time and there is a granddaughter to dote on. And yet Mark's enthusiasm for building something with his own hands, and growing corn on his own land, gives them a constant source of energy with which to carry their new mill forward. What they prove is that there is no such thing as a "standard" miller. Members of a new breed, coming to it late in life and doing it in their off-hours, they're working from a desire to produce something by hand that will last for future generations.

✳

Jim Barkley, owner of Barkley's Mill, is motivated by his own interpretation of the modern-day small family farm—as well as the fine art of product marketing. One indication that Barkley's is unlike most other mills is that they occasionally employ a publicist. Because of it, the mill and its products, which are produced by Jim's son-in-law Micah, have seen their fair share of press in a number of Southern food publications.

Jim and his wife, Iris, purchased a piece of land in Weaverville outside of Asheville, North Carolina, when their three daughters were still young. Jim owned car dealerships in the area and was looking for a place outside of town where he and his family could stretch their legs a bit. Originally, the property belonged to a family that had raised eight children inside one tiny cabin. When Jim found it, the cabin didn't have heat or running water, so he and Iris set to work fixing up the place.

The land around and behind the house is fairly hilly; a steep ridge juts upward a few hundred yards behind the home. But Jim saw an opportunity—there was enough cleared land that could be farmed. First they tried cattle, but the terrain didn't suit the large-hooved animals. Then he moved on to goats, but ran against issues with hoof management. Finally, they decided to expand what had been a family garden and take up the growing and milling of grains.

The land is suited for a mill. A narrow creek runs behind the original house, just downhill from the ridge, which is blanketed in white oak trees. In a broad divot of land, Jim positioned a dam, creating a pond in the stream. To the side of it, he built a water-powered mill wheel.

Though Jim had zero milling experience coming into the process, he's made up for it with enthusiasm. A born salesman, he sees it as an opportunity to build an agriculture-based business from the ground up. The mill and the building took years to cobble together; the clearing of land and a few years of experimenting with seed had been an investment. But his hope is to create a type of back-to-the-earth, sustainable lifestyle that he and his family can share. And while he's not the one tilling, planting, or running the mill, he considers himself to be the architect of a movement;

he's installed the infrastructure, complete with glossy marketing, that he, Micah, and their families can work within.

Jim's operation is thorough. He farms his own corn, having chosen the heirloom variety Hickory King because it has historically done well in that region, providing a good yield even in the hilly lower terrain of Appalachia. He grows it on two different plots, rotating his fields each year. And he's built a sturdy and reliable mill, choosing waterpower because it's a cleaner energy source—he also has solar panels attached to his corncrib.

Set just up the hill, the crib is inside an immaculate white barn, where tools hang neatly in a row and the solar panels are lined up along a length of the roof. In the barn's basement, an elaborate system of generators and electric paneling powers the system.

Inside the barn, Micah and his team shell the corn by hand, using a long, broad table and medieval-looking hand tools to pull the kernels away from the cobs. This hands-on approach allows them to sort out the "awfuls," or bruised kernels, from those that are going to be ground into grits or reserved as seed for next year's harvest. Between the hand-harvesting and the shelling, each piece of corn is likely touched by hand several times, helping to produce a consistent product.

The final piece of the puzzle is the millhouse. The building is the size of a tiny, two-story cabin, and prominently features a large, two-story wooden waterwheel. The building is Jim's pride and joy—one he's taken time and care to build. As water courses over the wheel, it fuels the intricate system of gears and pulleys set beneath the building, which in turn powers a dual mill system up on the top floor. The two mills are painted canary yellow with black trim and are fed with two chutes that hang like an upside-down Y, leading grain into each of the mill's hoppers. Beside them, a wooden bolter set with a metal screen is attached to the output of one of the mills—Barkley's Mill sells both bolted and unbolted product.

With all this infrastructure, it's clear that Jim sees bigger things to come—for now, producing a few thousand bags of grits each year (even at the astronomical cost of eighteen dollars for a two-pound bag of grits), plus whatever additional revenue they bring in from their merchandise, the numbers don't seem to add up. But Jim's greater desire is to create a more robust and sustainable system—he's already created multiple jobs for his family members, as well as others in the community, like the farm crew . . . and the publicist. What comes next will allow them to take the business to the next level: Jim wants to open a distillery on the property. Because he's taken his time setting up the system, from the planting and harvesting to the processing of the corn and, yes, to the marketing, he would do well wading into the high-yielding, high-profiting world of distilling. It would allow him to put the milling operation to use in a bigger way, while also providing even more jobs for the community—and it would ensure that this little plot of land continues to be used for agricultural purposes for a long time to come.

GRUYÈRE GRITS WITH WILD MUSHROOMS

Courtesy of Barkley's Mill

Serves 8

"The texture and flavor of nutty Gruyère cheese and wild mushrooms folded into our heirloom grits will remind you of risotto—but it's much simpler to make. The earthy flavor of this dish makes it a nice match with grilled pork chops or roast chicken. Or take a cue from risotto and serve it as a hearty main course along with a crisp arugula salad tossed with a tangy vinaigrette."

3 cups stone-ground grits, cooked

½ cup heavy cream or milk

1 cup grated Gruyère cheese

2 tablespoons butter

¼ teaspoon white pepper

2 or 3 shallots, cut into thin slivers (about ⅓ cup)

1 or 2 garlic cloves, finely minced

1 teaspoon chopped fresh thyme, plus leaves for garnish

8 ounces sliced mixed mushrooms (about 2 cups)

½ cup dry vermouth or white wine

Salt and freshly ground black pepper

In a heatproof bowl or serving dish, combine the warm cooked grits with the cream and Gruyère. Cover the bowl with a lid or foil and keep the grits warm while you prepare the mushrooms.

In a medium nonstick skillet, melt the butter over medium heat and season with the white pepper. Add the shallots and garlic and cook, stirring, until the shallots are translucent, 1 to 2 minutes. Add the thyme and mushrooms and cook, stirring, until the mushrooms begin to brown, about 2 minutes. Add the wine and simmer the mixture until most of the liquid has evaporated and the mushrooms are tender. (Depending on the mushrooms you're using, you may need to add more liquid and simmer a few moments longer to ensure they're tender.)

Fold the mushroom mixture into the grits. Taste for seasoning—you may need more salt. If the grits seem too thick, add a splash of water. If they've cooled down too much, reheat them in the microwave. Top with freshly ground black pepper and a sprinkle of fresh thyme leaves.

A Mess of Grits

While many of today's grits millers are putting up a good fight, not all of them are winning. In Belvidere, Tennessee, where the farm supply stores outnumber vehicles on the road, rising tree-covered hills make their way toward the Cumberland Plateau. Meandering streams and short waterways carve out hills and hollers that hide long-abandoned whiskey stills or still-intact historical markers. One of those markers stands in front of Falls Mill, one of the few remaining historic water-powered wheel mills, which remained in operation for nearly a hundred years, having shut down only recently.

John Lovett, the mill's proprietor, is a spry, trim guy in his mid-sixties who once taught industrial engineering in Chattanooga. Back when he was fresh out of graduate school, he met his wife, Janie, who was about to graduate with a degree in sociology and anthropology from the University of Tennessee at Chattanooga. John had long been fascinated with old machinery and the history of technology—mostly because he loved researching the machines themselves to find out who had designed and built them, when they were built, which parts and pieces made them run. Janie, meanwhile, was interested in how technology affected people's lives—an anthropologist, she was motivated to learn about the people who operated the machines. Together, they decided to start a museum that would be dedicated to the history of power sources and technology, which they founded as a nonprofit in 1981.

They were looking for a piece of property where they could house their museum when they came across Falls Mill. In the early 1800s, when the area was originally being surveyed for land grants, the spot was designated as a mill seat thanks to the nearly twenty-five-foot drop the stream took at that particular point. Early on, there were mills built nearby to support the growing cotton industry of Franklin County. There was also a community grain mill that sat a little upstream—the remains of the building are still embedded in the ground. When the Falls Mill site, a three-story brick mill building, was erected in 1873, it was originally used as a textile mill, operated by a large wooden waterwheel. In 1907, a thirty-two-foot overshot stainless-steel waterwheel was installed. At the time, it powered a cotton gin.

The rise and fall of textile milling brought the mill in and out of use—for about thirty years, it was used to turn woodworking equipment—until it was purchased by Colonel and Mrs. Woodrow Crum in the late 1960s. The Crums turned it into a grain mill, purchasing equipment from out of state and gathering parts and pieces from other mills in the area that had gone out of commission, to attach to the waterwheel's internal mechanism. When John and Janie purchased the mill, it had been a grain operation for only fifteen years of the waterwheel's long life.

Although the property was too expensive for the Lovetts, the owner eventually came down on the price, and Janie and John became the owners of the water-powered wheel, the mill, and the building in 1984—he was thirty-three, she was twenty-four. At the time, the mill was fully functioning, though the product offerings were slim—yellow cornmeal and whole wheat flour. Two millers, Adrian Gonsolin and his apprentice, Butch Janey, had been operating the equipment at Falls Mill since it was installed in the late '60s. The Lovetts both kept their day jobs in Huntsville— John as a professor of industrial engineering at the University of Alabama, Huntsville, and Janie as a travel agent—and let the millers continue their work during the week.

The couple joined SPOOM, the Society for the Preservation of Old Mills, an organization that gathers like-minded people who own or operate old mills. They were among the youngest members at the time—but the resources and community proved essential as the couple got to know their aging acquisition. Meanwhile, Butch kept the mill running; the Lovetts would come up on weekends to clean up the space, package and ship the product, and ready their museum—many of the museum's artifacts came from the property itself.

Soon they were able to grow the milling operation, as well as the product line. In 1986, their miller made the suggestion that they start packaging and selling grits, so they purchased a bolter from Meadows Mill. Once the system was installed, the grits immediately took off; their first major restaurant client was Magnolia Grill in Charleston, and with a little word of mouth, production grew from there.

Over the thirty-plus years the Lovetts ran the mill commercially at Falls Mill, they went from a retail and mail-order business to supplying more than two hundred wholesale and restaurant clients all over the US. They were milling about a quarter million pounds each year, using corn grown in fields nearby, and brought to the mill by the wagonload.

The heart of the Falls Mill operation was, and still is, the massive, thirty-two-foot overshot waterwheel. The stainless-steel beast seems to sigh and groan as it makes its lazy, circular rounds. At the very center, there's a pinion, the main spoke that enters the building. The wheel lets off a woodsy fragrance of old moss, worn-down metal, and fresh spring water. Its creaking joints and steady motion produce the lull of a sleep-inducing white noise machine. As the gears and belts work their way into a dance, the whole building seems to come alive once the system of belts and wheels starts churning, gaining momentum, as well as enough energy to power the stone-grinding mill, which is inside, close to the wheel's mechanisms.

The wheel has 112 miniature buckets, each suspended evenly between the wheel's rims. Several feet upstream from the mill building, the water is captured and harnessed at a high point in the creek. A narrow channel, called the millrace, collects the water and directs it past the mill building and over to the top of the wheel.

To power up the wheel, one opens a gate in the millrace, letting water from the stream rush down the channel toward the wheel, where more gates, powered by a system of levers, control the water flow. It takes about ten minutes for the millrace to fill, and once it does, the gates to the wheel are opened, allowing just the right amount of water to spill into each tiny bucket. It's not the force of the water but the weight that causes the wheel to spin at its even, lazy pace.

In 2001, the rocks of the millrace, and the rock wall that supported it, partially collapsed—it took a mountain of concrete and a small fortune to restore it—and most of the work fell on John, who had learned to fix just about any problem that came up at the historic property.

The wheel's back-end mechanism runs the height of several stories. From the point where the pinion enters the wall and upward, the belts, mostly made from sturdy cloth or leather, whir around their various-size wheels. The belts flap around silently, like duck feet paddling through water. The entire system is an engineering marvel—a rhythmic, almost hypnotizing act of continual motion.

Inside the building, all of that power is being directed to the mill itself, which looks like a massive hat box set atop a sturdy wooden base. Inside, two forty-two-inch granite burr stones—weighing 2,100 pounds each—sit horizontally. The stones are cut, or dressed, with ridges that counter one another so that as the top stone turns, anything caught between its ridges, and those etched on the base stone, gets crushed. The ridges act like scissors, so depending on how close or far apart the stones are set, corn kernels, which are fed into the stones through a hole cut into the top stone, are milled into large and small pieces. Another hole in the bottom stone sends the milled corn down through a shoot, and into a wooden bin attached to the side of the mill.

The stone burr mill was originally built by R. D. Cole Manufacturing in Newnan, Georgia, sometime around 1900. Though John ran it two or three times a week for decades while the mill was in operation, it now sits quiet, a relic marked with signs, as part of the museum's aging collection.

In 2015, the FDA made a surprise visit to Falls Mill—Janie was giving a tour to school children when they arrived. The agents spent two days examining every facet of the business, eventually telling the Lovetts they had about two weeks to either modernize the space with sealed walls and doors, or stop production altogether. The Lovetts decided to cut bait.

Their lives are much different now than they were when the mill was running. The wholesale business was so good it paid for the mill, and for a full staff. Eventually, they even bought a farm, about 90 acres, nearby. They credit their first restaurant client, Magnolia's in Charleston, which had a cooking school, for a majority of their wholesale business, since a number of Charleston's most prominent chefs first heard about Fall Mills through the school. They hardly even had to advertise.

Looking back, John misses the money. And Janie, who had good relationships with a number of chefs, misses those relationships. The day the FDA showed up, she was filling an order for Magnolia's and told the chef what was happening—he was distraught over losing his supplier of fresh-milled grains. Neither John nor Janie, however, miss the dust or the noise or the boxes.

The bigger issue for John is trying to decipher what prompted the FDA to come after such a small-time, historical operation. The whims of whichever political entity is currently in power can dictate where the FDA focuses its attention—perhaps, he believes, in that particular moment, it had sway from someone attached to the industrial food giants. But the technology of milling has been in use for thousands of years—so why, suddenly, would an operation like Falls Mill have to shut things down? Nobody, as John likes to point out, ever died from eating bad cornmeal.

Today, the museum and store are still in operation and the Lovetts run a bed-and-breakfast out of a log cabin that sits on the property. Though the mill no longer produces grits, Janie and John still turn the ancient, creaking, overshot mill wheel most days. Falls Mill grits and cornmeal still exist, processed and custom-labeled at Logan Turnpike Mill in northern Georgia. It keeps their brand name out there and allows them to have some product for their store, as well as the small handful of restaurant customers they still supply. In their retirement, John and Janie are still proudly peddling grits. And they continue running the museum, which sees a few thousand visitors each year.

In this carved-out little Tennessee holler, living in a log cabin, the Lovetts may have lost one battle—but through their efforts to protect and preserve the past, they're still standing on the front lines and, in their own way, contributing to the ongoing fight against a fully industrialized food system.

EASY CHEESE GRITS

Courtesy of Falls Mill

Serves 4

1 cup Falls Mill stone-ground grits

6 cups water

1 onion, thinly sliced

2 teaspoons instant chicken bouillon

2 tablespoons butter

½ cup half-and-half

2 to 4 ounces American, cheddar, or Havarti cheese, grated

Place the grits in a bowl and cover with 2 cups of the water. Stir so the light bran rises to the top; carefully pour off the water and bran, reserving the grits in the bowl. Rinse again if desired.

Combine the remaining 4 cups water, onion, instant chicken bouillon, and butter in a heavy-bottomed saucepan. Bring to a boil and stir in the grits. Reduce the heat to low, cover, and cook, stirring occasionally, for 20 minutes, or until the grits are soft and creamy. Add the half-and-half and cheese and stir until the cheese melts. Serve hot.

❧

FRIED GRITS

Courtesy of Falls Mill

Serves 4

1 cup Falls Mill stone-ground grits

6 cups water

1 teaspoon plus 1 tablespoon salt

1 tablespoon butter

1 cup all-purpose flour

2 teaspoons freshly ground black pepper

1 cup vegetable or canola oil

Place the grits in a bowl and cover with 2 cups of the water. Stir so the light bran rises to the top; carefully pour off the water and bran, reserving the grits in the bowl. Rinse again if desired. Combine the remaining 4 cups water, 1 teaspoon of the salt, and the butter in a heavy-bottomed saucepan. Bring to a boil and stir in the grits. Boil for 1 minute, then reduce the heat to low, cover, and simmer, stirring occasionally, for 20 minutes, or until the grits are thick and creamy. If they're too thick, add a little more water or some milk or cream.

Pour the cooked grits into an ungreased loaf pan and let cool until the grits are firm, 30 minutes or more. Invert the pan onto a cutting board so the loaf of grits slides out. Slice crosswise about 1 inch thick. In a shallow plate, combine flour, remaining 1 tablespoon salt, and the pepper. Dip the grits slices in the flour mixture to coat both sides.

Heat the oil in a high-sided skillet over medium-high heat. Fry the floured slices for about 5 minutes per side, until golden brown.

The Chef Activist

Opened in Nashville in 2007, City House restaurant arrived at the beginning of what would become a tidal wave of coolness washing over Music City at the time. I first read about the restaurant in *Bon Appétit*, where restaurant editor Andrew Knowlton included them in several glowing write-ups, including a piece about how he discovered a new side of Nashville while riding alongside musician and producer Dan Auerbach of the Black Keys. In the piece, Andrew likened the opening of City House to the broader movement that was turning food into a progressive statement in the South; he wrote that a chef like Tandy Wilson, who ran City House, could move things forward in a city's, and region's, dining culture.

At the time, a growing number of pockets across the South were gaining attention for creating strong microregional identities. No longer grossly generalized as a pan-Southern region—one where biscuits were served on every plate—the South was now being recognized for its many regional cuisines and foodways, and many chefs were contributing to the revitalization of those traditions that helped define specific cities, counties, islands, and hollers.

That microregional exploration has continued at a breakneck speed, with chefs, cooks, beverage experts, farmers, writers, and product makers all diving deep into a very specific territory to uncover and put forth the identity of a place, helping each location stand apart in a multistate region.

In Nashville, chef Tandy Wilson, a born-and-bred local, was a founding member of the movement. Having worked in California and fallen in love with Italy through his travels, he'd found a kinship between Italian and Southern ingredients. Channeling his grandmother, whom he called Nana Crick, Tandy often likened the elements and traditions of both regions in his cooking—he started by spinning Italian-inspired fare out of Southern ingredients, which he had come to respect deeply. The wood-fired ovens that sat just beyond a tiled dining counter in his restaurant pumped out blistered pizzas topped with belly ham. Freshly made pastas like *strozzapreti* were ladled with turnips and octopus ragù. His grits, which appeared in several iterations on the menu, were cooked *al forno*—in the oven—and nestled with a cauliflower ragù and ricotta.

Though his restaurant opened a few years before the city saw a crush of new businesses that would turn Nashville into an "It" city, Tandy set a foundational standard against which all other rising restaurants would be measured. The crowd that showed up in droves—musicians, politicians, emergency room doctors, Belle Meaders, academics—found equal footing at the table, all dining on Tandy's comforting yet boundary-pushing food.

Set in an old artist studio, the room is simple—high ceilings, exposed ductwork, industrial metal chairs slid under wooden tables. The first time we ate there, Dave reveled in the stellar bourbon selection while I eyed the pepper-flecked belly ham pizza, which came with the option of an egg on top. From my seat, I could see into the shotgun kitchen space and watched the chefs behind the line, many covered in facial hair, some with tattoos. It struck me how calm and genuinely happy everyone appeared—from the fast-moving chefs to the casually dressed servers. Their relaxed demeanor signaled a genuine joy for being in that place.

Shortly after starting down the path of writing about grits, I had a meeting at City House, where a few of us gathered for a drink and a snack. On the menu, I spotted a dish called sour grits cake. A friend had mentioned to me that Tandy was milling his own grits, so when the chef stopped by our table to say hello, I asked him about his mill. He pointed to a machine sitting directly in front of the host stand. "A Meadows mill. I got it about a year and a half ago," he said. I dug for a few more details: Where was he getting his corn? How often did he mill? Finally, I put out a feeler. "Next time you run up to the farm to pick up your corn, could I come with you?"

Sure, he replied. "Anytime."

A few weeks later, I let myself in through the kitchen door of the restaurant and found Tandy at the bar fiddling with the espresso machine. He had to put a stock on to boil but would be ready soon, he said. In the meantime, I caught up with Rebekah Turshen, the restaurant's talented pastry chef, who was sipping a cup of coffee. We chatted about a shortcake recipe she needed to send me for a magazine story and I asked her how things were working out with the restaurant's mill. She was using the cornmeal in a lot of the desserts, she said, including that shortcake recipe.

Soon Tandy was ready. We stepped out into the chilly May morning, jumped into his weathered pickup truck, and hit the road.

On the half hour drive to Orlinda, Tennessee, toward Windy Acres Farm, which was his source for the corn he was milling, I asked Tandy why he'd decided to start milling corn at the restaurant. He said he'd been paying attention to the conversation that had been building lately around grains—how they've become so manipulated, being bred and grown for mass production while steadily losing flavor. News reports about genetically modified foods and books like *The Third Plate* by chef Dan Barber were becoming a bigger part of his daily intake. And then he was invited to cook a dinner in Philadelphia with chef Marc Vetri at the restaurant Vetri, where he saw the chefs in the kitchen milling corn into polenta on a small, countertop Meadows Mill machine.

"I'm a hands-on type of person—doing it yourself really forces you to take on something that maybe you don't fully understand. At Vetri, they happened to be using this Meadows mill, and sometimes, you see something at work and you see great people getting great results—immediately, it was like, 'That's the right decision,'" he explained.

Not to mention that he was about to lose his own grits supplier. "We got our mill and we'd maybe run it for a week or two when the letter came in the mail that Falls Mills was done," he said. The historic water-powered facility in Belvidere had been supplying City House with its grits for years, so the news came as a shock to Tandy and the hundreds of other chefs who sourced grits and other products from Falls Mill.

"It was sad as hell—but the whole thing has been a little telling of our situation. Because that happened, and suddenly, we were scared to use any grits because we never knew how much we might be getting. And now we've found Windy Acres, so we know where to get our corn. Now it's 'How much do we need to yield five gallons of grits today? Let's get the mill out.' We don't run out of grits or cornmeal now," he said. "We just run out of corn."

As a kid, Tandy ate grits out of a box. "Maybe quick, but probably instant," he admitted. But even without a personal reference point for the flavor of stone-milled grits, he said, he remembers the flavor of real cornmeal that his great-aunt Kay and her sister, Nana Crick, used. "They grew up in the country and always talked about what they had in the family larder," he said. His own cornbread recipe is almost exactly the same as his grandmother's.

Putting the mill in the restaurant was not, he said, a way to recall the grits of his youth, because frankly, those quick and instant grit memories weren't worth holding on to. Instead, he was discovering the true flavor of corn, and playing with grits and cornmeal in new ways.

The sour grits cake that I had eaten, he said, was modeled after Italian *farinata*, a thin pancake or crepe made from chickpea flour. His sour grits cake had a similar texture and flavor profile. "It's paper-thin, crispy, and sour, and there's a certain mush familiarity at the center of it," he said.

For a regular dish of grits, he wasn't messing around, either. "It takes about three hours to cook 'em," he said. "I want to know the cracked corn is in there, but it better be creamy. I don't want any starch around it, I don't want to crunch on anything. I think it's offensive to have undercooked grits. In this part of the country, you better get that right."

As we pulled off the highway, I asked about the process of milling and how much time that took.

"It's incredibly labor-intensive," he admitted. "And if you think about the cost and what's going on the plate, it's extremely difficult for me. This is food that, traditionally, we ate for sustenance, something everyone could afford. Now, all of a sudden, I'm putting it in a fancy bowl and charging fifteen dollars for it. That's a hard thing," he said. "But what we're really doing here is supporting Windy Acres by milling their corn—we are saying this food system is broken. I'm not going to put up with instant grits. If that was my only choice, we wouldn't serve grits. I hope City House is priced as low as it can be while still making sure that everybody that works there makes a good living."

Price point was something he considered constantly. A lot of people, including those who live in the low-income neighborhoods that surround Nashville's Germantown neighborhood, where his restaurant is located, can't afford to eat his food. But he rationalized it by explaining where the money went. First, to pay for the corn, sourced from a local farm; and to pay for the time-consuming labor of hand-milling and separating the grits, which meant cash in the pocket of one of the three chefs who work in the kitchen each day. In the case of the sour corn cake, served at the time with a chicken sugo, there was also a three-day souring process; the price of the buttermilk, made by a farmer in East Tennessee; the price of the chicken, also sourced locally; and the cost of the other ingredients that went into the sauce. The chain went on and on. So the fifteen dollar price tag of the dish reflected far more than just the cost of a plate of food. It reflected a larger ecosystem that Tandy was trying to support through his work—one where the dollars were spread, as much as possible, throughout his local community.

We arrived at Windy Acres and pulled past a simple farmhouse where two huge fuzzy dogs ran excitedly across the yard. Behind the house sat a barn and an open-sided storage structure. The land opened up beyond that into a vast maze of fields set on more than 450 acres, most of which were farmed organically. At one end, the very early tops of a new crop of corn were just starting to jut out of the ground.

We met Holden, a dark-eyed farmhand who welcomed Tandy with a firm handshake. He showed us into the storage space where a mammoth two-story grain cleaner took up one corner of the structure. Holden thought it dates back as far as the 1930s or '40s, and said it was now mainly used to get the cockleburs separated from the corn, soybean, and wheat they were growing.

Just then, Alfred Farris, founder of Windy Acres, sauntered over. White-haired, tall and lean, he wore a thick Carhartt jacket and a wide-brimmed hat. Standing erect with his hands in his pockets, he looked like he might be out for a nature walk. He moved with purpose and a steady gait.

Tandy introduced us and asked Alfred to talk me through the operation. They'd been farming since 1986, he said. There were the grains—yellow and white corn, soybeans, wheat—but he also had a herd of about seventy cattle, which he called a critical part of cropping. They rotated the cattle and the crops every three years, allowing the cattle to graze and fertilize a section of land before it was planted.

I asked Alfred about the corn Tandy was buying, which he called Jubilee. "About fifteen years ago or so, there was a corn breeder at Cornell and he probably knew more about open-pollinated corn than anyone else I've known. He traveled all over the world, to the Andes, getting to know these ancient corns. He wanted to help farmers develop strains of open-pollinated corn that could be commercially viable. So he offered to help us. He got a set of parent seeds and showed us how to cross-pollinate it, which we did by hand, with just a little garden plot and a little handful of corn. Out of that, we've kept that corn and that's what you're getting now. We call it Jubilee corn—there is no patent on it. All the seed companies, they want to develop a patent, but we see it so differently. Here it's a life form, so it shouldn't be patented," he explained.

For Tandy, the story of Jubilee was essential—but so, too, were the properties that made it a great grits and meal corn. He liked the color and the heft of the kernel, which shone like sunshine when it peeked out of the tall, fifty-pound brown paper bags that he purchased. He paid Holden for two bags that day and slid them into the back of his truck before we waved our good-byes.

As we pulled away from the farm, Tandy told me that what he'd really like to see is a few other restaurants buying corn directly from Alfred. "I want to help him out, and I think if I can get just a few others on board, we can make it work. He doesn't have a distribution plan. It's just got to be a few of us, running up here when we can and picking up bags for the group," he said. The look of determination on his face made me think it wouldn't be long until he'd made that happen.

A few weeks later, I headed back over to City House, this time to watch Tandy mill. On the menu that week, he was doing a crispy grits dish, which was almost like the sour grit cakes I'd tried before. But this time he was cooking the grits, then letting them set in a pan before slicing them into small rectangles. Right before plating them, he slid a pan of the sliced grits into the kitchen's wood-fired oven, where the tops of the cakes got crispy brown. The grits came out with a crunchy crust—Tandy served them alongside sweet corn, pickled peppers, and cucumbers for a taste of summer on a plate.

When I arrived, Tandy was pulling the mill from its perch near the host stand. It was set on a rolling cart that had been rigged specifically for the mill, with a hole under the mill's output. Once he'd set it up near the kitchen, he set a bowl on the shelf underneath to catch the milled grains. On top, a plastic funnel was used to feed the whole kernels into the mill. Before doing anything else, Tandy wiped the machine down with a cloth and added a little grease to the gears. Then he walked into the kitchen to grab a fifty-pound bag of Jubilee corn, similar to the one we'd picked up a few weeks before. He poured a stream of canary yellow kernels from the bag into a white bucket and sifted through them with his hands.

"We used to have to blow the chaff off, but now that they have that new separator you saw, we don't have to do anything to it," he said, picking over the kernels with care.

Back over by the mill, he fired up the machine. A loud, high-pitched rumble ambled out, filling the entire room. Tandy lifted the bucket up to the top funnel and poured some of the corn in. Away it fell down the shoot, jittering into the body of the mill.

The mill was round and compact, a sleek white contraption. Underneath it, I could see a poof of powder emerge and then the dusty milled grains start to pour into the bowl. A few more minutes went by and Tandy pulled the bowl out slightly so I could peek in. The golden, flour-like results looked as soft as sand.

After he'd milled the full batch, he took the bowl over toward the kitchen, where he'd already set up a second bowl and a round, 8-inch metal sifter. He poured a heap of the milled grains onto it and start shaking it lightly, banging the contents around until the larger grits were jumping around on the screen. It was the same maneuver I'd seen Lawrence Burwell use at Congaree—only Tandy wasn't using a vacuum to pull out the pericarp.

"Seems awfully involved," I said, watching him work.

"We call it tedious." He laughed. "Your eyes start to cross if you do it long enough."

Of the batch he was producing, he said about 60 percent would end up as grits and the other 40 percent would make cornmeal for Rebekah's recipes. With that, he pulled out a measuring cup and filled it with exactly 1 cup of cornmeal. He walked it over to Rebekah, who stood at her pastry station readying a few ingredients. She smiled brightly and took the measuring cup from him.

"How often do pastry chefs get to work with freshly milled meal?" Tandy said, nodding her way. One cup of cornmeal, a bowl of dry-ground grits, and the show of support, however humble, were his tools. As an activist chef, he wasn't going to let the many influences of Big Agriculture or industrial food take him down. He was a mobilizer against the system—using grits as a potent political weapon to fend off the big food beasts, one plate at a time.

CITY HOUSE SCRAPPLE

Courtesy of Chef Tandy Wilson

Serves 6 to 8

"We usually serve this with a vegetable slaw or fresh salad with acidity to complement the scrapple."

1 cup grits, soaked overnight and drained

4 pounds pork butt, cubed

1 pound pork skin, cut into small pieces (have your butcher do this)

35 grams salt (about 2¼ tablespoons)

2 tablespoons freshly ground black pepper

5 garlic cloves, chopped

3 cups white wine

Preheat the oven to 325ºF.

Combine all the ingredients in a baking dish with a lid. Cover and bake for 3 hours. Let cool to room temperature.

Line a loaf pan with plastic wrap. Transfer the cool baked grits to the bowl of a stand mixer fitted with the paddle attachment and whip for 2 minutes. Pour the grits into the prepared loaf pan and let set in the refrigerator for an hour or more, until chilled.

Use the plastic wrap to remove the loaf of grits from the pan and discard the plastic wrap. Cut the grits into 1-inch pieces and pan-fry them. Serve with slaw or a fresh salad.

A Plate of Grits in the Cultural Mix
The Chefs, Cooks, and Eaters Honoring Grits Across the South

Excuse me. Do you eat grits?"

Through a camera lens, a blonde with a curly bob smiles. "Yes, I eat grits. I *loooove* grits." She giggles.

In the 1978 documentary by Stan Woodward called *It's Grits*, a montage of scenes unfolds with a narrator off-screen approaching people to ask them how they feel about grits. First the film is focused on Southerners. But then, as the story unfolds, there's a pivot, and the camera is on the streets of New York, where it encounters a less-friendly reception. Most of those faces don't know about grits—one man bundled completely in a fur-lined hooded coat, asks, "You mean, like, crackers?"

And then: a man in an overcoat, well-groomed, standing on a busy New York sidewalk and speaking with a slightly affected accent:

"You know what's really good?" he says. "It's a grits soufflé. Made with sharp cheddar cheese and eggs, and the egg whites beaten stiff and folded in. It stands way up like that and it's just about, I think, my favorite way of eating grits."

The narrator asks who he is.

"Yes, my name is Craig Claiborne and I'm the food editor of *The New York Times*. Eternally in search of good food, I've been around the world numerous times, but I still go back to the food of my childhood."

The scene cuts to Craig standing in a kitchen, tying on an apron as he explains what to do: Add one cup of grits to four cups of water.

The camera moves in close on Craig's face as he talks about growing up in Sunflower, Mississippi, his face nearly filling the frame.

Cut back to the aproned Craig, standing beside a stove and whisking grits in a pot. "The grits are ready in about five minutes. They become quite thick. Then we add to them a half cup of milk or heavy cream."

In a voiceover, he continues: "It's about time these Yankees woke up to the good things in life."

Stan Woodward, who also documented the stories behind the camp meeting sites in South Carolina, released his film as an experiment—a form of capturing first-person stories in an unconventional (at the time) handheld camera style, where the focus came in and out, and shadows crept into odd parts of the black-and-white frame. Viewers journeyed with Stan as he held his camera up to a person to ask them how they felt about grits. It also marked another important turning point for grits, during which the dish was making moves beyond the previously mentioned "Grits Line," and out into a national consciousness.

The film was released two years after Jimmy Carter was elected to the presidency. "Gritz & Fritz in '76" buttons had become icons of Carter's ascension. And on the television show *Alice*, Flo was already cracking up audiences with her famous catchphrase, "Kiss my grits!"

Grits, in those days, were mostly found as a mass-produced breakfast product found in boxes on grocery store shelves, thanks to large brands like Quaker Oats, Jim Dandy, and Aunt Jemima. Grits had already made their way north, and could be found all over the country.

Craig Claiborne, whose mother ran a boardinghouse in Mississippi, started writing about grits in *The New York Times* in the 1960s. In a brief article called "Concoctions with Corn," published in 1965, he wrote, "Of all the abundance of corn products—corn meal, grits, hominy, and the like—only corn meal seems to have a national appeal. More's the pity, because both grits and hominy can be delicious—once a taste for them is acquired." He included a recipe for "Grits Casserole Texas-Style."

In 1967, he went deeper, reporting on a grits-focused luncheon, complete with antebellum undertones, like women wearing hoop skirts, that was hosted by Quaker Oats at New York's Carlton House, "to introduce the fine-grained cereal to recalcitrant, stubbornly rebellious Yankee palates. It is a missionary effort not unlike, perhaps, teaching a Southern cook to turn off the heat when the greens are done."

In that piece he dropped data about the consumption of grits: at the time, 85 percent of all grits sold were purchased in the southeast, mainly to an eleven-state region from Texas to the Carolinas; Southerners were consuming four pounds of grits per person each year. He then listed a recipe for "grits and cheddar casserole," which, he noted, "is conceivably the most talked-about recipe in the Southeast."

By 1976, Craig was ready to proclaim that grits were moving north. Spurred by the presidential nomination of a Democratic Southerner, he noted that grits could be found almost everywhere. Recipes printed alongside that piece were adapted from a collection of Southern cookbooks, including the *Christ Church Cook Book*, compiled by the women of Episcopal Christ Church in Savannah, Georgia, and *Cane River Cuisine*, gathered by the Service League of Natchitoches, Louisiana.

It wasn't until 1985 that Craig put his most notable rubber stamp on a dish involving grits. It was the year he published a piece about a young chef from Chapel Hill, North Carolina, named Bill Neal. The piece, "For a Carolina Chef, Helpings of History," offered a warm and thoughtful profile of the up-and-coming force behind the restaurant Crook's Corner, as well as a recipe for Bill's "Shrimp with Cheese Grits."

A Tale of Two Bills

Bill Neal didn't invent shrimp and grits, but he had the biggest hand of anyone in reviving it. From behind the stove at Crook's and through the words of Craig Claiborne's article, the dish seemed to alight into the culinary canon, appearing on restaurant menus across the South almost instantly. Chef Robert Stehling, chef and owner of Charleston's Hominy Grill, got his start working for Bill and, after a stint in New York, went down to the Holy City to open his own restaurant in the '90s. Though he'd worked in Charleston long before, and had never once seen the dish on restaurant menus back then, suddenly, there it was—shrimp and grits—at every important restaurant in town. Open since 1996, Stehling's Hominy Grill has served grits from the beginning. The chef, who grew up in North Carolina eating stone-ground grits, put a shrimp and grits dish on his menu right away, working from the same style of recipe that he learned while working at Crook's.

The dish has roots in the Lowcountry, where first mentions referred to it as "shrimps and hominy," hominy being interchangeable with grits for those living in that area (even though not all "hominy grits" have been made from a nixtamalized corn product) and was eaten in the morning, with the shrimp being freshly caught from a creek or stream during shrimp season, and sautéed for just a minute, maybe with a little salted water, before going on top of a pile of grits. These were home-prepared meals, not found in restaurants. Recipes for them didn't appear in newspapers until 1891.

Lowcountry food authority John Martin Taylor, who goes by Hoppin' John, grew up in Orangeburg, South Carolina, near Charleston; on weekends, he'd be on a sailboat with his family, exploring the Sea Islands and eating his way through the Lowcountry. John grew up setting out shrimp nets and collecting oysters near the pluff mud. His family would bring "country grits," a stone-ground alternative to the mass-produced boxed product of the 1950s, onto the boat with them each weekend—after catching shrimp, they'd cook them up with a thin sauce and call it "breakfast shrimp."

(Later, John opened a culinary bookstore in Charleston called Hoppin' John's and, after some research, realized that no one was selling the grits he remembered eating as a kid. Determined to find a way to get some of those grits of his childhood back into his life—and sell them in his store—he connected with several millers who were stone-milling grains, including George and Cecilia Holland, who owned Logan Turnpike Mill in North Georgia. At the time, they were growing their own corn and milling it. John started selling their grits by the bag in his bookstore, first under the Logan Turnpike label and then under his own custom brand.)

Theories abound on how creek-caught shrimp and grits first came together. At the 2016 Southern Foodways Alliance Fall Symposium, Michael Twitty spoke about a number of things, including his take on the argument about whether sugar belongs in corn bread. (He believes it has long been there, in the form of molasses, which an enslaved person might have gotten as a ration.) During the talk, he boldly declared, "I don't care what anyone says, shrimp and grits came from Mozambique." The statement came with backup—he told of dishes from that country involving corn and shellfish, a combination that he said appeared before those in Charleston were eating it for breakfast.

Other notions about how and where it became popularized can be made. For example, in New Orleans, also a port city where various cultural influences merge and mingle, a listing for "breakfast to-morrow" in the May 8, 1895, edition of the *Times-Democrat*, the menu included "Fried Lake Shrimp. Grillade. Hominy."

Greg Johnsman of Geechie Boy likes the theory he once heard about how the fishermen and oystermen of the Lowcountry, some of his wife's own ancestors, would often go out for long hauls—twelve- or twenty-four-hour stretches—which required them to bring any necessary provisions out with them on the boat. They'd call it a one-pot, carrying a single pot that contained all their food for the trip. Grits or rice, both cheap and filling staples, would go into the pot, as would whatever they were catching that day. Shrimp, a major provision for South Carolina fishermen, would get tossed into the pot, along with a little seawater, and all of it—the grits or rice and shrimp—would cook down to a simple, filling meal. Cheap, nutritious, substantial, and sensible—and just as likely a point of origin as any other out there.

But it was Bill Neal, a white chef raised in rural North Carolina, who took inspiration from that original combination of ingredients—shellfish and ground corn—and created a dish that became cemented in American cooking.

Growing up in Grover, North Carolina (population 400), Bill was exposed to food through the rural traditions of his family. His grandparents lived off the land and had fruit trees in the yard; it was a childhood of hunting, gathering, foraging, and gardening. In his book *Bill Neal's Southern Cooking*, he remembered discovering freshly caught quail, still warm, in his father's coat pockets, and tiny radishes his sister grew each February. There was an uncle Skinny who trapped terrapin, and pickled peaches at Sunday dinner. He also noted that it took going abroad to understand that some of the rituals of Southern cooking were as important as those found in other cultures, and worth the time and effort to celebrate.

Bill went to Duke University in the early '70s, where he met his wife, Moreton. The two cooked together in her dorm room, and during his junior year, Bill took a job as a server at a restaurant that sat between Chapel Hill and Durham. Together, the couple explored food everywhere they went, including New Orleans during trips to Moreton's hometown in Mississippi—they'd take the train down to the city to eat for the day.

Later, Bill went back to graduate school, but on the side, started cooking in restaurant kitchens. There were trips to Paris. The couple's son, Matt, was born. And in 1976, Bill and Moreton opened La Residence at Fearrington Village near Chapel Hill. They lived on the property in what Moreton described as "life in a fishbowl," with any home cooking mostly being an experiment for the restaurant, and the cast of kitchen members who were coming through the house being treated like family.[15]

In her look back at Bill's life, Moreton described him as "seductive," "unconventional," and living "as if there were no tomorrow." These same qualities, she wrote, "made up a recipe for marital disaster." Plus, it turned out, Bill was gay. The two divorced in 1982, and she continued to run La Residence while he moved on to open Crook's Corner.

Like any good Southern landmark, the space now occupied by Crook's Corner has a storied past. Once owned by a Mrs. Crook, who was mysteriously shot, the building was established in 1941 as a fish market. It went through a few iterations before falling into disrepair. Later, it became a pool hall, a gas station, and a barbecue joint, until Bill and his partner, Gene Hamer, turned it into a full-service restaurant.

At first, Bill cooked the same kind of food he'd been preparing at La Residence—European in tone and style. But in 1984, a knock on the door caused him to rethink his direction altogether.[16]

It was Craig Claiborne, who had come to town to research an article for *The New York Times*. As Moreton explained, "Bill was invited to lead this powerful tastemaker on a tour of barbecue joints in eastern North Carolina towns. [. . .] After spending time with Mr. Claiborne, a Mississippian by birth, Bill found that his vision had come into focus. 'The South has at least as much as California to offer,' he told Mr. Claiborne. Bill envisioned a niche that nobody had filled, and he moved in that direction."[17]

Shortly after that first visit with Mr. Claiborne, Bill went on to begin researching his book. He left Crook's for a while to do his research, and it was during that time that Craig returned, sitting in Bill's home kitchen while the chef cooked shrimp and grits and the journalist captured the recipe.

In 1991, Bill Neal passed away, a victim of AIDS. He'd written four books, including the *Good Ole Grits Cookbook* with Bill Perry, and had moved from cooking passionately and experimentally with a focus on foods from the South of France, to redirecting both a personal and national conversation toward the foods of the American South and its culinary traditions.

Before departing, he influenced countless other chefs. Of those who worked in his kitchen and alongside him, Robert Stehling (Hominy Grill, Charleston), John Currence (City Grocery, Oxford, Mississippi), and Bill Smith (Crook's Corner) would all go on to pick up the mantle and continue shaping the dialogue around Southern cuisine.

Today, Crook's Corner is a room trapped in time with black-and-white-checkered tiling around the bar, black-topped metal-rimmed tables set without linens, and sturdy vinyl chairs. Local art, sometimes pop-inspired, sometimes photographic, hangs on the walls. There's kitsch in the form of hand-thrown pottery pieces on the bar and tacky pig art on the walls. A James Beard Award hangs quietly amid it all.

Printed on plain white paper, the daily list of dishes is placed between plastic sleeves, the date listed at the top. Summer might find main dishes like a tomato tart, or a plate of pan-fried bluefish. Sliced fresh figs topped with slivers of cured ham. Cold buttermilk and pinto bean soup. A watermelon-and-tomato salad. Honeysuckle ice cream and Atlantic Beach pie. And there are classics, like overstuffed deviled eggs, fluffy and filling hoppin' john, a side of cheese-laden water-ground-style Moss White Grits, and a cracker plate with pimento cheese that gets a dash of bourbon. This is still a spot where Southern food is prepared and served simply—not overdone, not experimented or tampered with. Simply, Southern favorites—equal to or better than your mom used to make.

The shrimp and grits is a busy-looking pile of food. The bacon seems abundant, but so, too, are the mushrooms, big slices of mottled brown. A lemon, meant to be squeezed over the pile, garnishes the plate. The pink edges of shrimp peek out, revealing just the faintest crust from a quick turn in a hot pan. The taste of the grits is buried beneath it all, prevalent with cheese.

It is still the same recipe that Bill Neal placed in front of Craig Claiborne more than forty years ago—minus the nutmeg, chef Bill Smith will tell you. The recipe in Neal's cookbook has nutmeg, which the restaurant doesn't use. The only other change has been the grits themselves. Originally, Crook's sourced from Adluh in Columbia. Now they use the water-ground Moss White

Grits from Buffaloe Milling Company, right up the road in Kittrell, North Carolina.

In his uniform of faded, worn-out T-shirt and ball cap, Bill Smith has become an essential fixture in the Southern culinary story, too. A native of New Bern, North Carolina, Smith grew up the eldest of five always surrounded by fantastic food, cooked by his great-grandmother, grandmother, and aunt. He was drawn to music and eventually went to Chapel Hill for college, where he gravitated toward the city's music scene. He helped open the Cat's Cradle, a small and now legendary rock club. He took jobs as a server at a few spots, lived in a big house with a big group of friends, and, as he says, "had a big old time."

It was while looking for some extra cash so he could get himself to Europe that he started cooking—he picked up a job chopping parsley and peeling potatoes at La Residence under Bill Neal. When he returned from Europe, he went back to La Residence and stayed, working with Moreton after Neal left to open Crook's. Later, a few years after Neal died, Bill Smith took over Crook's, where he's been hanging out in the kitchen for nearly twenty-five years.

On a visit to Crook's Corner, Bill once presented me with a clear plastic zip-top bag full of dry white grits. One of the restaurant's regulars, Jack, had found some corn seed awhile back. He'd grown it out in his garden, milled it by hand, and brought it over to Bill that morning. "He thinks the seed was about fifteen years old, probably a variety called Old Haney," he said. The words "grits coarse" and "5 lb" were scrawled on the bag.

Bill cooked up a pot of the grits and came out a short while later holding a small dish of grits and two spoons. A pat of yellow butter melted temptingly down the sides of the mound.

He sat beside me, set the bowl between us, and handed me a spoon. We both dug in, watching the steam float up from the still-hot pile, and chewed thoughtfully on that first bite. We looked at each other, nodded, and *mmm*'d. "That's got a lot of flavor right up front," he said.

I tasted the way the butter coated the corn, enhancing the starchy pile. I could feel the faint crunch of the bran, still mixed in with the grits—it wasn't enough to get stuck in my teeth but it was a sure sign that these had been hand-milled.

We sat there together, each spooning up bite after bite, sharing our small bowl of grits. Like all those grits lovers in Stan Woodward's *It's Grits* documentary, our nods of approval were the only indication an onlooker needed to see how much we appreciated the plate of grits between us.

❄

The stories of Bill Neal, Bill Smith, and Crook's Corner are well told and revered by many Southern chefs. There are tributes to Bill Neal's cooking across the South. In Nashville, there's a dish at the restaurant Biscuit Love, owned by chefs Karl and Sarah Worley, called the Bill Neal, which is Gulf shrimp with cheese grits, fatback bacon, mushrooms, scallions, and Tabasco. (The Worleys' grits get a good solid splash of half-and-half.)

The dish has also gone on to take many different forms. The original Neal recipe has been replicated and redone, but it's also been turned on its head, spiced up, and dismantled or deconstructed, depending on where it's gone—which is far and wide.

There are Creole versions, like one found at Seattle's Toulouse Petit, which puts fat, wild, Pacific-caught, head-on shrimp in a sauce that gets loads of black pepper alongside housemade andouille sausage and bits of crawfish—the creamy corn grits serve as a cooling antidote to the spice. In Charleston, tomatoes get thrown into the mix, which is why Husk does their rendition with peppers and onions that are braised with tomatoes and their juices. At Ida B's Table, a modern soul food restaurant in Baltimore, chef David Thomas uses Anson Mills grits and slathers his shrimp in a creole cream sauce, topping it all off with pork belly croutons.

This doesn't even scratch the surface of other, similar dishes that replace the shrimp with a variety of other proteins. Grits and grillades, stewed medallions of beef, is a traditional New Orleans dish that can be found at breakfast or dinner. And the blending of cultures occurs in Houston where chef Chris Shepherd of One Fifth and Georgia James might put a red chile–braised Wagyu barbacoa over Hickory King grits.

All of these versions are worth seeking out—but the shrimp and grits dish crafted by Bill Neal, and still prepared exactly the same way by Bill Smith, stands as the hallmark, despite its likely African roots.

The timeline of the trajectory of shrimp and grits, which came to prominence in the hands of white male chefs at a time when Southern food was rising in popularity, means that like so many other dishes, it still carries with it the weight of appropriation— an unfortunate fact that still deserves reckoning. Around the time that Neal was sitting down to cook for Craig Claiborne, chef Paul Prudhomme, who had already opened up the palates of New Orleanians, was taking his show on the road to cook in

San Francisco and New York, bringing Cajun spice, andouille, and blackened fish to diners around the nation.[18] Louis Osteen brought oyster stew to his restaurant in South Carolina. Frank Stitt opened Highlands Bar and Grill, giving Birmingham, Alabama, its first fine-dining temple to elevated Southern fare.[19] As these chefs gave attention to the home-cooked dishes of earlier generations, they gave American consumers the sense that the identity of the South was changing. Grits, once a cheap and lowly cereal product, was now a symbol of forward progress—and yet, served alongside shrimp and fancy gravy, also served as a masked example of the region's continued strife. And soon it would move from reinvented home cooking to experiments in molecular gastronomy.

SHRIMP AND GRITS

Courtesy of Chef Robert Stehling, Hominy Grill

Serves 2 to 4

Chef Stehling pulled inspiration for his dish directly from his time working with Bill Neal at Crook's Corner. There's no nutmeg, but otherwise, it's a close replica to the recipe Craig Clairborne printed—and it's what Stehling serves at Hominy Grill every day. But, he adds, it can be simplified. "Older Charlestonians will sometimes see this as really complicated and ask me to do plain shrimp in butter—I know exactly what they want," he says. "At its simplest, the dish can be just plain, pan-fried shrimp with grits."

3 slices bacon, chopped

Peanut oil (if needed)

1 pound shrimp, peeled and deveined

2 tablespoons all-purpose flour

1¼ cups sliced mushrooms

1 large garlic clove, minced

2 teaspoons fresh lemon juice

½ teaspoon Tabasco sauce

¼ cup thinly sliced green onions

Cheese Grits (recipe follows), for serving

In a medium skillet, cook the bacon over medium-high heat, stirring occasionally, until crisp, 5 to 6 minutes. Drain the bacon on paper towels, reserving about 1½ tablespoons of the bacon fat in the pan; add peanut oil, if needed, to make this amount.

Heat the bacon fat over medium-high heat. Toss the shrimp with the flour until they are lightly coated, shaking off any excess flour. Place them in the pan and cook until starting to turn pink on the first side, then flip the shrimp and add the mushrooms and bacon. Cook for about 2 minutes. Add the garlic, stirring continuously so as not to brown it. Remove from the heat and add the lemon juice, Tabasco, and green onions. Spoon into bowls over cheese grits.

CHEESE GRITS

4½ cups water

1 cup stone-ground grits

1 teaspoon salt

¾ cup grated sharp cheddar cheese

¼ cup grated Parmesan cheese

3 tablespoons butter

½ teaspoon freshly ground pepper

½ teaspoon Tabasco sauce

In a medium saucepan, bring the water to a boil over high heat. Whisk in the grits and salt, reduce the heat to low, and cook, stirring occasionally, until the grits are thickened, 35 to 40 minutes. Remove from the heat and add the cheeses, butter, pepper, and Tabasco. Taste and adjust the seasonings as desired.

The Innovators

When it opened in downtown Birmingham in 1982, Highlands Bar & Kitchen was an anomaly. Few restaurants in that city, or extended region, were latching on to French sensibilities, let alone shaping their menus with a farm-to-table ethos. But the chef, Frank Stitt, a native of nearby Cullman, Alabama, was twenty-eight years old and, emboldened after a year spent in Europe working as an assistant to cook and food writer Richard Olney, a gig he'd gotten after working with Alice Waters in Berkeley. Both experiences had strengthened his belief that Southern food could be elevated with fresh, regional ingredients and French techniques, and that a restaurant experience could be elegant, casual, hospitable—and might even offer a sense of humor.

One of the dishes that landed on his original menu was called stone-ground baked grits—it's still on the menu today. Tongue firmly planted in cheek, Frank listed the dish as a simple appetizer, but what came out on the plate left diners awestruck. Frank pulled from his mentor, Olney, who inspired a Swiss-style, twice-baked soufflé. The grits, which he was getting from the only source for stone-ground grits he could find at the time, a nearby health food store called Golden Temple, were blended with a good bit of Parmesan cheese and whisked with eggs to make a sort of custard that was then baked. Around it, he pooled a sauce of sherry vinegar, reduced down with a fistful of shallots, thyme, and country ham trimmings, which was then whisked with an unmentionable amount of butter and more Parmesan. Julienned slices of country ham and sautéed mushrooms topped the dish, along with a shower of fresh thyme leaves.

This fantastic and fanciful version of the dish, along with the rest of Frank's menu, swiveled heads as far away as New York, putting Highlands on *Esquire*'s Best New Restaurants list two years later. This was just around the time Craig Claiborne was revealing the magic of Bill Neal and his grits-based shrimp dish at Crook's Corner. (To be fair, Frank's baked grits showed up before Claiborne's Neal article.)

Today, the stone-ground baked grits are the same, if just a bit more refined. Frank now uses a technique for tempering the eggs into the cooked grits, causing the custard to maintain an ethereally feathered texture that seems to just whisper across the teeth before liquefying on the tongue. The country hams are less salty and the mushrooms are sometimes foraged. But otherwise the Highlands grits dish is precisely as head-swiveling now as it was thirty-five years back.

Frank, like many, grew up eating grits but didn't necessarily enjoy them. "This was the sixties, so most grits were industrial—Jim Dandy, you know. So there wasn't a particularly good quality about them or even good things to say," Frank told me on one of my visits to Highlands. But the discovery of stone-ground organic grains at the local health food store helped him unlock a new level of flavor in the breakfast staple. Eventually, Frank tracked down the miller, based in North Carolina, and started sourcing directly from them.

In the decades since he started making the dish, Frank has worked with only a handful of grits producers. His discovery of Glenn Roberts and Anson Mills in the early 2000s was a game-changer. Suddenly, Frank saw an opportunity to elevate grits without adding much to them, and incorporated them into his menu as a side dish or an accompaniment to proteins. With Anson's grains, he could make a simple porridge cooked down with water (and only water, Frank insisted, stating that cooking them with cream or milk made them "just too overly rich") and a little salt. He still uses Glenn's Pencil Cob grits, putting a spoonful of them alongside fish or roasted meat, or preparing them as a side dish and crafting them into a grits cake.

But he'd also found a local supplier in McEwen & Sons, which sat just a few miles down the road from Birmingham in Wilsonville. The miller, Frank McEwen, whose family owned a farm-supply store, started milling corn after inspiration struck his father during a trip to Sevierville, where he saw a water-powered grist-mill turn corn into fresh stone-ground grits and cornmeal. He brought bags of the stone-ground grits home, planting a seed in McEwen's mind. Later, after a health scare, the family made the decision to move to an organic, high-fiber diet and stone-ground organic grains became a priority. They weren't easily accessible at the local grocery, so, around 2001, McEwen bought a Mead-ows mill and started milling organic corn into grits, cornmeal, and polenta, for his own use, and also to sell in his farm-supply store.

To build up an audience, McEwen also wisely delivered a few samples to restaurants around town, including Highlands. A short while later, Highlands started ordering them regularly—a fact that McEwen believes helped seal his fate. Just like that, McEwen & Sons grits were named on the Highlands menu and Stitt's cus-tomers, who at that time, hailed from points around the country and globe, became aware of the farm-supply store miller of Wilsonville, Alabama. Soon McEwen had chefs from Seattle, New Orleans, and New York calling to place their orders.

Frank McEwen's store stands off of one of Wilsonville's main roads. Farms and pastures dot the hills that surround the town—Frank Stitt now owns his own farm just a few miles away; he buys his farm equipment, as well as his chickens, and many eggs for his restaurants at McEwen's Coosa Valley Milling and Hardware store. The white Meadows mill Frank McEwen uses is set up in a contained room attached to a storage facility near the store, along with a shimmying eccentric sifter. The system puts out grits and meal and, like most good milling operations, is lightly coated in a thin white corn dust. Inside, the room smells of corn, sawdust, and fuel.

Though Frank McEwen doesn't create custom grinds or work with heirloom varieties, his organic grits are a go-to for chefs around the country—a fact he credits entirely to Frank Stitt. "He's like a godfather to this business, and to my sons," he told me. "I owe him a lot."

❄

In 2011, Atlanta chef Linton Hopkins flew out to the Culinary Institute of America campus at Greystone in Napa Valley for the annual Flavor Summit. As it is every year, the gathering was a who's who of chefs, restaurant executives, and bar experts, and Linton was there to demonstrate a dish he called "Georgia on a Plate."

Before the conference, Linton was chatting with Sean Brock— both are big fans of Anson Mills and the cold-milling techniques Glenn Roberts uses to lock in the flavor of his grains. The two started brainstorming ways they could apply similar techniques to certain foods and the topic of liquid nitrogen came up. At the time, Linton was trying to figure out the whole liquid nitrogen thing—did it really improve food and flavor, or was it just a gimmick? He took the idea out to Greystone to find out.

Standing before an audience of curious eyes, Linton put a pile of fresh hominy that he'd sourced from Anson Mills into a bowl and poured liquid nitrogen over the top. The nixtamalized corn froze up immediately. (Linton had practiced this a few times and knew, after busting a few blenders, just how frozen the corn needed to be.) He then transferred the frozen corn to a Vitamix blender and whirred them up into tiny, pebble-size granules. He put the resulting grits into a pot over a low heat and added just a little bit of water to reconstitute the mix.

"The process turned the grits into this amazingly soft-textured dish that was also super creamy and so full of flavor. They were almost velvety," Linton recalls. By eliminating the drying process and skipping straight ahead to the act of "milling," he'd managed to preserve and even enhance the texture and flavor of the corn, while also elevating the expectation of what people were about to eat.

On the plate, he sidled a small pile of the grits next to a sorghum-glazed slab of pork belly and a tuft of baby collard greens. The results astounded everyone in the audience, which included Anson's Glenn Roberts. "I have to say that besides eating grits made by a Native American, out of a clay pot, those were the best grits I've ever eaten," Glenn told me.

Southern chefs, Linton explained to his audience that day, were certainly stewards of the past—but they were also always looking for new ways to do things. Hence using this uber-modern technique on such a humble style of food. He also noted that, if he were to name the dish *guanciale con polenta*, he could charge $50 for the plate. But if he listed it as hog jowl and grits, people would balk at paying just $3 for it. "Georgia on a Plate" was an attempt, he said, to restore respect for the old foodways—and for a dish that is too often associated with poor people and poor food.

Through his various Atlanta restaurants, including Restaurant Eugene and Holeman & Finch, Linton sources grits from a number of Georgia and Alabama purveyors, relying heavily on whichever chef leads each kitchen to seek out and select their own sources. Through these channels, he's discovered Red Mule Grits, milled by an older farming couple who literally power their creaking ancient mill with the slow gait of a red mule. There's also Riverview Farms in North Georgia, where the Swancy family grows their own heirloom corns and miller Brad Swancy grinds them into meal and grits on a Meadows mill. At Holeman & Finch Public House, when chef de cuisine Spencer Gomez has Riverview Farm grits on the menu, he might ply them with black pepper and a drizzle of sorghum syrup.

Linton is also still a fan of Anson Mills. He met Glenn around 2004 after opening Restaurant Eugene. "Glenn and I started having these conversations about how grits are not really grits. I mean, I was born and raised in Atlanta, I grew up in a classic Southern home. We ate grits, probably from Aunt Jemima, or something, but I had no concept of sourcing. I had no memory of where things really came from. So meeting Glenn and just learning that there were even two different types of corn, dent and flint? It was all new to me," he told me.

Today, Linton is not only educated but, like many Southern chefs, he's on a newfound and continual learning journey, and regularly aims to apply "old-school" techniques to his cooking. Lately, he's even started making his own hominy. More than a decade after those first eye-opening conversations with Glenn, he's become a conversation-changer of the New South—a chef who has tapped into the new style of Southern cuisine while constantly attempting to channel its history. His high-tech experiment at Greystone only moved grits, and our perception of it, forward.

e☆9

GEORGIA GRITS

Courtesy of Chef Linton Hopkins

Serves 4

Grits

3 cups local heavy cream

1 cup local milk

1 cup coarse-ground grits

1 teaspoon hot sauce

Kosher salt

Sorghum Butter

1 pound (4 sticks) butter, at room temperature

¼ cup sorghum

Kosher salt

Freshly cracked black pepper, for serving

MAKE THE GRITS: In a medium saucepan, heat the cream and milk until warmed and beginning to steam—do not allow to boil. Slowly add the grits, stirring continuously. Cook for 20 minutes, or until the grits are completely hydrated and tender. Some grits may require a little more liquid as they cook. If needed, heat the milk in a separate pan before stirring it into the pot with the grits. Season with the hot sauce and salt and keep warm until ready to serve.

MAKE THE SORGHUM BUTTER: In the bowl of a stand mixer fitted with the paddle attachment, beat the butter on medium-high speed until creamy and white. Add the sorghum and salt. Mix on low speed until incorporated.

To serve, spoon the grits into small bowls and place a pat of sorghum butter in the middle of each. Season with freshly cracked pepper.

While grits have traveled far and wide, one area still boasts what is likely the highest concentration of restaurants serving grits, and that is the jut of land that makes up Charleston. Restaurant critic Hanna Raskin keeps a blog for the city's paper, the *Post and Courier*, and wrote to a curious reader: "Should you notice differences among the grits you try, that's likely not the kitchen's doing. Rather, the characteristics you're bound to pick up on—such as sweetness and texture—are determined by the mill. The most respected milling operations in South Carolina are Anson Mills; Allen Bros., which makes Adluh Stone Ground Grits; and Geechie Boy. When those names show up on a menu, that's a green light to proceed down grits avenue." For a more signature Southern experience, she notes that she particularly likes the smothered pork chop served with grits and toast for $6.50 at Hannibal's Kitchen, "one of the last remaining soul food restaurants on the peninsula."

After Hoppin' John opened his culinary bookstore in the 1980s and started peddling stone-ground grits, chefs in that town, like many around the country, began to embrace the use of local, artisanally produced grits. When Robert Stehling was making his shrimp and grits dish at Hominy Grill, starting in 1996, he brought in grits from the historic Old Mill of Guilford, North Carolina, where his own family had bought them when he was growing up. And later, when restaurants like Husk started touting their purveyors on menus, the popularity of small-batch, stone-ground grits surged. Now the early efforts put in place by Hoppin' John have finally borne fruit—today, just about every new restaurant that opens in Charleston, it seems, is putting stone-ground grits on the menu.

On the corner of Upper King and Mary Streets, which is now part of the city's bustling restaurant row, the Darling Oyster Bar opened in 2016. The airy space took over the bottom floors of one of Charleston's 115-plus-year-old two-story storefront buildings. Against the exposed red brick, white tiles, and wood trim, a muted sea green marks the stool tops and banquettes, putting a timeless appeal on the energetic space. Along with a lengthy list of oysters served on the half shell, they also serve a side dish of grits with red pepper relish. The pile of speckled porridge comes thick with corn particles and a pile of shiny, finely chopped peppers and onions that have been bathed in vinegar and sugar to complete the tart relish finish. The overall effect is balanced, with the saltiness of the grits comingling with the tartness of the relish.

A few blocks away, the Rarebit is a modern, all-day diner on King Street. In their side dish of grits, the melding of tangy cheeses and a heavy dose of hot sauce give the grits an extra oomph of flavor.

There are grits being put into a beer at Charleston's Revelry Brewing Co. And grits might come brûléed in a custard at Mc-Crady's.

When Greg Johnsman of Geechie Boy opened his breakfast-and-lunch spot Millers All Day in Charleston with chef Nathan Thurston, one of the first newsy tidbits to come out about the restaurant was its "unicorn" grits. The corn, bred by a farmer in Appalachia, was pulled from the random red kernels that can appear on a yellow ear of corn. The farmer collected only those random kernels until he had enough to plant. The corn kernels are pink all the way throughout and, when they're milled, offer up a soft pink hue. Images of these unicorn grits flooded Instagram, giving Johnsman and his team a quick boost in regulars right out of the gate.

All of these versions of the original humble dish are a tribute to and evolution of the grits that Native Americans painstakingly prepared centuries ago, then handed over to colonial settlers. Though the preparation has gotten easier, and the prices people pay to eat them have skyrocketed into a previously unimaginable range, grits in all forms still serve the purpose of comfort and sustenance.

Grits for a Crowd

As with countless other iconic foods, there is no greater validation of a people's love for grits than the celebration of it in festival form. There are a handful of grits-related festivals now, including the National Grits Festival in Warwick, and the Shrimp and Grits Festival on Jekyll Island, both of which are in Georgia. And at the annual World Grits Festival, held for more than thirty years in St. George, South Carolina, each spring, the love and passion people have for grits is brought vividly to life.

There are plenty of reasons to make your way down to

St. George for the festival. One can eat grits, and watch other people eating grits. There are grits-eating competitions, in fact. And there's plenty of people-watching to be done when thirty-five-thousand grits lovers drop into a tiny town for a little slice of Americana.

But the most fascinating aspect of the annual event, and the main reason I attended it one year, has to be the grits roll. The World Grits Festival has been taking place along the same sleepy strip of St. George every spring since 1985—the grits rolling started up shortly after the festival's inaugural run. My primary interest in making my way that first time was to see the spectacle of people rolling in the grits.

This celebratory weekend-long event, started by those thoughtful marketers behind the local Piggly Wiggly, has waxed and waned in attendance over the years. Quaker Oats, a longtime sponsor, had for years contributed its name, financial support, and, of course, plenty of grits for the event. Quaker's sponsorship dollars went specifically toward the festival's marketing and advertising budget. And they also donated product, including thousands of single-serve disposable bowls of instant grits, in flavors like redeye gravy and ham and cheddar, as well as all the boxes of product needed for the grits roll, which amounted to almost two thousand pounds of dry grits.

During the festival weekend I attended, which started with a prayer breakfast on Friday morning, there were arts and crafts to peruse, bands and dancers to enjoy, an hourlong parade of floats and cars on Saturday morning, a 5K fun run, Hula-Hoop and basketball contests, a dunking booth, and, of course, grits-based meals to savor. The meals were prepared and served by members of the New Grace United Methodist Church, who battered and fried up slices of catfish and chicken and served them on plastic plates alongside a spreading pile of grits. I ate mine with a tomato gravy that smothered everything on the plate, after squeezing a few lemon wedges over it all.

The meals were served at the back of the World Grits Festival headquarters, a long narrow building that the festival committee purchased back when the event was in its prime. It sat near the western end of South Parler Street, smack in the center of the festival activities. The front of the building, cut into a main room and some administrative offices, was wallpapered in snapshots and Polaroids taken over the years, showcasing children and pageant girls, contestants from the grits-rolling contest, and members of the committee that aged as the images moved down the wall. There were a couple of folding tables set up in the room acting as a retail store. They were blanketed with T-shirts, hats, and other souvenirs, like pocket-size bags of grits and buttons, all emblazoned with the festival's logo, a simple and smiling farmer in overalls and a straw hat waving a World Grits Festival flag and an ear of corn.

The back of the building was a long dining hall with a kitchen at one end. The walls of the hall were lined with clotheslines where a rainbow of children's art hung, all of it themed around grits and the festival. Organized by the St. George Women's Guild, the art show was a point of pride, each crayon and colored-pencil work contributed by local elementary school children. Ribbons proudly proclaimed the art contest winners.

Since the beginning, a handful of active locals have carried the festival on their backs through volunteer service each year. It started with John Walters, one of the owners of the Piggly Wiggly, who acted as festival chairman. He ran it for the first two years but then turned the baton over to Roger Myers, who still holds it today. Nell Bennett was probably the festival's most recognizable face. Known affectionately as Granny Grits, she became the heart and soul of the event, acting as the ambassador and central PR figure. Nell owned and ran an appliance store in St. George, and was an active member of the community—so much so that the town named a street after her. And because of the festival, Granny Grits came to be interviewed internationally, appearing on NPR and in the pages of *The Wall Street Journal*. When she gave up her position in 2002, it left a hole in the planning committee. When she passed away in 2005, the entire town mourned the loss, showing up to fill the family's refrigerator with food for weeks.

These days, the prominent faces on the steering committee included Steve Franks, who'd originally told me about the camp meeting sites—he'd been volunteering at the festival for twenty-seven years and "ran the street," renting out space to vendors, organizing the tents, and so on—as well as Frances Fralix, a no-nonsense organizer who worked by day as a tourism coordinator for the Tri-County Regional Chamber of Commerce but whose primary role over the festival weekend was running the on-site store, managing the T-shirts, printing up brochures, and securing the dance squads that performed each year. There was also Roger Gaither, who worked with a marketing agency in Mt. Pleasant and helped secure the sponsors and celebrity hosts each year.

Though he wasn't an "official" committee member, Philip Ranck might well have been the most important man on site. Philip ran and managed the production of the rolling in the grits contest, preparing the activity from top to bottom. He was the man I'd gone to see. His procedure, which I staked out like a hawk throughout the weekend, started around eight thirty a.m. on Saturday morning, right around the same time the runners of the Grits Festival 5K fun run were doing their last-minute calf and neck stretches along the sidewalk in front of the World Grits Festival headquarters. Philip, who lived a few towns over in Summerville, was one of the only paid members of this mighty tribe. Somewhere in his thirties, Philip had a squinty gaze, unevenly cut hair, and one large buck tooth, which popped out between his lips every time he smiled.

That morning, he began his procedure by blowing up an eight-foot-long inflatable pool using an air pump. The pump was neither high-powered nor efficient, so it took almost a full thirty minutes, the air loudly spewing into the sides of the pool. Philip looked on, bored and restless.

By the time the first runners were coming over the finish line at the end of the race—the line sat directly across from the semi-truck trailer and Astroturf-covered platform that acted as the stage for the grits roll—Philip had gathered a stack of boxes, each full of five pounds of Quaker Quick Grits, original flavor. I wondered what made the quick grits a better fit than, say, an instant variety, and soon understood that the quick grits allowed for slower absorption—it was a lengthy process to get all of the grits emptied into the pool and then mixed with the water. Instant grits would have puffed up too quickly.

Philip was patient in his opening of each box, and in his dumping maneuver. He slid his finger across the box lid, pulling back the flap and pouring the grits out slowly. He'd been doing this long enough—fifteen years, to be precise, with a few years of training before that—to know that this process would take up his entire day, and that he'd be earning a full day's salary for it, thanks to Quaker. And so he was deliberate in his movements, except when he was tossing the boxes toward a large trash bin—the thin cardboard pieces occasionally trailed off with the wind, landing outside of their intended target.

After emptying a dozen or so boxes, Philip started up the hose. He began by adding water in stages, not all at once or after each box. It was somewhat scientific in that he knew he must stir the grits and the water together at certain moments so as not to create too much resistance. He used a finely carved rowing paddle to mix the grits. Like a canoe paddler, he held his hands at the top and middle of the paddle, dipping the flat end into the middle of the pool and pulling it toward himself in short, deep strides. He walked from one end of the pool to the next, pulling and dipping, occasionally letting the paddle stand to see if the grits had thickened up. With his hose nozzle set to mist, he'd sometimes spray the edges of the pool where the grits had snuck up along the sides, like they do in a burbling pot.

He was still adding dry grits to the pool when the parade, which started at eleven a.m., began to pass him by. There was the first float, which carried the Grits Sisters, a tidy gang of straw-hatted women who were members of a local bridge club—a club so tight, and so fiercely proud of their role as Grits Sisters, that the women didn't allow new members unless one of them passed away. At least that's what one of the Festival organizers whispered to me as she trailed behind them in a golf cart. "Practice up on your bridge skills, you know, just in case one day . . ." She laughed, puttering off with a nod. I nodded right back and threw her a thumbs-up.

Philip occasionally took a break from the stirring to wipe his forehead. His World Grits Festival T-shirt stayed remarkably white and starched, but his faded baggy blue jeans started to show signs of his duties toward the very bottom where a light coating of grits had formed. The black sneakers were thick with a crust of grits and every now and then, he stomped his feet to shake off the caking corn crust. When he did take a break, the mixture settled a bit, leaving a few inches of water pooling over the grits, like that moment when you put too much water in your oatmeal and it separates discouragingly. The grits, at this stage, were thick but continued absorbing the water, as though the molecular compounds attached to the corn product might expand exponentially until the pool simply burst, allowing the grits to overflow into the streets. It didn't, of course. But the whole contraption seemed capable of anything without Philip's care and attention to the task.

By about noon, Philip was adding the last box of grits. The empty boxes were hauled off the stage and the crowds were filling the streets, many munching on whole barbecue turkey legs and cotton candy cones twice the size of a person's head. The smells filling the air weren't, as I had imagined, grits-y. Rather, they were smoky, heady, and sweat-infused. Philip was sweating, too, but kept calm, continuing his short strokes of stirring, hands gripping the paddle tightly.

The first round of grits rolling would be the kids' category. Children aged six through fourteen were invited to sign up in advance. Roger Gaither, the go-between agent for the title sponsor and the festival, managed the back end of the grits roll and so he was in touch with all of the parents of the participants in advance, giving them some guidance and instruction. The goal of the grits roll was to accumulate as many pounds of grits onto your body as possible. Contestants would be weighed on a scale that got zeroed out as they stood on it, before jumping into the pool of grits. They would have ten seconds to roll and then be weighed again to see how much weight they'd accumulated in grits.

That year, none of the kids who were to participate had done it before, so Roger offered his advice. There was the outfit, which required some planning. Fleece and fleece-like materials offered up the best sticking surfaces and coverage areas, meaning the person could accumulate more grits poundage. Contrary to what one might think, grits don't stick very well to skin or hair. Yes, it helped to dunk your head into the mess and give it a good rub, but what you really wanted was to load up the pounds in your clothing. Tape the ankles with duct tape. Tape the waist, too. Savvy kids wore a pair of pants that were about ten sizes too big, taped them at the ankles, and put on suspenders, so that, like a clown, they could fill up their pants to a comical expanse. Wearing a hoodie was wise, too, especially when turned backward so that the hood was in front, creating a trough-like catchall for the sticky white substance.

Before the contest got under way, Philip, who had finished filling the pool with a whopping seven hundred pounds of dry grits, stood at the edge of his masterpiece. The grits were officially ready, he announced after standing his paddle in the center of the pool to see that the wooden stake had not budged. "It could be a bit warmer out," he muttered in Roger's direction. "But it'll work." He shrugged, removing his paddle. "We're ready."

Philip beckoned for the first set of contestants to join him near the stairs leading up to the stage. A large man wearing a straw hat manned the scale, which stood at one end of the pool—he was the official weight keeper of the grits roll. Philip led the first contestant over to the scale to get weighed in and then he and Roger lifted the young child up and placed his feet into the pool of grits. While this was happening, a couple of radio DJs who were there to emcee the activities, got the audience to count slowly up to ten.

The crowd was anxious. They booed and hissed when the first child didn't actually roll in the grits but rather, in an attempt to load up on pounds, scooped them into his clothing. But then, when the second kid, outfitted with pants duct-taped at the ankles and goaded by a stage mom who scream-cheered him from the side, took a headfirst dive into the scrum and rolled around joyfully, the crowd squealed in delight. The rolling looked difficult. The grits were thicker than mud and hard to maneuver in. But "Bubba!" as his mom called him, was round, with a full head of shiny, brown hair, and reveled in his roll, maximizing his ten seconds by piling grits onto his head and rubbing them around with glee. After ten seconds, Roger and Philip each took him under an armpit and lifted him up, placing him atop the scale. A twenty-two-pound difference, the weight-keeper exclaimed. The crowd screamed ecstatically. Later, Bubba would walk offstage with a small pile of cash for his efforts, his stage mom wrapping him up in a bear hug after the win.

What the crowd couldn't see was what was happening behind the stage. After each child took their roll, they'd walk down the stage steps and over toward a fence where, shivering against the late spring chill, each contestant was hosed down like an elephant at the zoo. The hose nozzle was turned to a forceful spray, in order to get the grits out of the places where it was bound to stay for days, maybe months, like inside the ears, down the gullies and valleys between their limbs, and stuck underneath the creases of their eyelids. The hose could not fully rid a person of the grits. Some contestants stripped down almost completely, or at least shed a top layer of their grits-catching get-ups. Some were prepared with whole new outfits—maybe there was a change of underwear. Some were not prepared at all and simply walked around wearing their soaking wet clothes, the grits crusted to them like cement. I saw a few water-logged kids scrambling to find sunny patches along the street where the heat was likely to dry them faster.

Most of the contestants would walk away with no cash prize money. The ones who did left beaming.

All the while, Philip took his duties seriously. Any time a kid was placed into the grits, he'd whisper a few last-minute tips in their ear. As they began to roll, his hand would go into motion, waving at them to roll more. His body involuntarily twisted as though he were the one rolling, as though his torso was the one being covered in grits. He mimicked them, clapped for them, and then, when the time was called, he was the first to reach out a hand to save them. Hero of the grits-rolling people. More than thirty kids competed that day, and he could probably tell you what each one did wrong or right. One didn't roll enough. One rolled enough but couldn't get the grits to stick. The ones who did it well earned a high-five from Philip.

When the grits roll was over, the crowd thinned quickly. The pool stayed where it was, about two hundred pounds lighter thanks to all the grits the kids had taken with them. Behind the stage, a pile of grits surrounded the spot where the children had been hosed down, rivers of the stuff spilling into the street. Philip stepped away from the stage for the first time that day and took a breather as he waited for a tractor to arrive and haul off the pool. All of it—the pool, the grits, the resulting mess—would go off to a hog farm, where the happy animals would devour every remaining bite.

On Sunday, Philip began his day in the same exact way, this time adding more grits to the pool for the adult competition. It was a more serious set of competitors on Sunday—those who took the grits-rolling seriously. If you chose to stand in the first row or two at the World Grits Festival during the Sunday adult rolling competition, you would walk away wearing some grits yourself. The cash prizes were higher that day, too. The winner, who managed to pile on forty-six pounds that year, walked away with several hundred dollars.

"Where else in the world can you spend ten seconds and win hundreds of bucks?" Philip asked rhetorically.

This remarkable ritual impressed me. There was an audience that literally, and figuratively, devoured this rowdy celebration of all things grits. Most of the attendees came from out of town, but the core group of regulars and traditionalists were from right there in St. George. It was a community that, year after year, honored the rituals set in place by the people before them in order to pull off an event that would draw out those who wanted and needed a place to gather, to eat grits, and to revel in a little friendly and harmless competition. This corner of the South, set at the cross-roads of the Lowcountry, near the Gullah Geechee corridor, near the stately charms of Charleston, near the white-sand beaches of Hilton Head, near the small-town Piggly Wiggly, showed a true picture of the South in all of its complicated and prideful glory.

To me, it was also a symbol of the pure and true power of grits. Each person attending the festival had their own story to tell of how they'd gotten there and why they ate, or didn't eat, grits. There were those who cooked and ate grits at home every week, buying theirs from the Piggly Wiggly in those round cylinder containers for $1.99. There were those who attended, and often cooked, at the nearby camp meeting sites, filling the bellies of all who gathered for those local, long-standing traditions. There were those who preferred their grits prepared at Narobia's Grits & Gravy down in Savannah, smothered and soulful. And there were those who ate them at fine-dining restaurants in dishes shaped like cones and swimming in an herbal broth.

This simple plate of food, which called to so many and brought them out en masse, encapsulated the high, the low, the right, the left, and everything in between of the South. To me, it was all wrapped up into one big, glorious mess—and it made me love the region, and the dish, that much more.

As the weekend came winding to a close, and the festival volunteers were doling out their last single servings of grits, the second inflatable pool full of grits was carted off to the hog farm. And that's when Philip really rested. He'd gone through a few

T-shirts over the course of the weekend, and they went into the trash, as would his jeans at the end of it all.

The black sneakers though, would stay. After stomping them a few times, Philip eventually took them off and gingerly banged them together several times to get the thickest part of the crust removed. But he wouldn't throw these away, he told me. These, he would keep. They would go out into his backyard.

"The only way to get all the grits off," he said knowingly, "is to put them on top of a red ant hill. Those fire ants, see, they eat all the grits right off that shoe. The shoe will be clean once the ants eat all those grits. And then," he said, grinning, "those ants will puff up and die."

Epilogue
Grits on My Table

While I researched and reported for this book, I stopped trying to count the number of bags of grits that filled my freezer—until, that is, in the middle of the project, when I carted about twenty bags with me as we moved from a small two-bedroom cottage into a roomier house on an acre of land a few miles away. I realized then that twenty bags of grits is far too many for any family of four to keep at any given time, no matter how often grits are served.

But instead of excess baggage, I looked at these packages of ground corn as both mementos from my own journey, as well as a welcome challenge in the kitchen. They became a puzzle piece for me to apply in a variety of dishes that stretched far beyond the basic breakfast casserole.

I'm a meal planner—mostly as a way to bring sanity to my family's weekly routine. But I operate that way only with the understanding that plans are often made to be broken. So if I decide on Sunday, before heading to the store, that I want to make a grits casserole to refrigerate and eat on Tuesday, that plan usually stays in effect until the offer of something more exciting, like the chance to dine at a newly opened restaurant for research purposes, pops up. The casserole will get eaten eventually, so I try not to stress too much when plans change. But at least I'm comforted in knowing that there is a plan in place, and when everyone does eventually get hungry I've got something homemade for them to eat.

Over the two years it took to research and write this book, grits became a regular part of our home diet. I usually tried to put grits on the breakfast table at least once each weekend. And on weeknights, I'd get playful, subbing out other carbs (pasta, mashed potatoes, rice) for grits to make up dishes like grits jambalaya, or a style of lasagna that layered meat ragù over piles of grits. Any dishes that called for polenta were fair game, so there were several nights when the house was filled with those rustic Italian scents of sausage, rosemary, tomatoes, and garlic—and grits were simply the vehicle.

Not every dish was a winner. There was a too-runny tomato sauce poured over a pile of undercooked grits that resembled a grainy bowl of pig slop. And there were the casseroles I overcooked, by accident or neglect, including one that required the trashing of a white CorningWare casserole dish after no amount of scrubbing with Brillo pads could remove the crusted-on mess.

But for the most part, I discovered grits made a fine substitute for many wheat-based staples that once filled our pantry. The timing on this was good, too, because halfway through my research, Dave started to take note of his own diet and specifically how gluten was affecting him negatively. We experimented by removing all gluten from his diet for a full month—the grits casserole and jambalaya went into heavy rotation—and he immediately dropped 10 pounds, plus a small portion of the inner tube he'd been carrying around his waist for a decade or so. He quickly noticed that the "stomach issues" he'd had for years disappeared almost overnight. The lack of gluten didn't seem to make much of a difference on my metabolism—but I was willing to pull most of the wheat-based products from our fridge and pantry if it meant that Dave would feel better on a day-to-day basis.

I also made attempts to practice the tried-and-true. I really wanted to master shrimp and grits, a dish that I'd eaten and fallen for over and over again across the South. From a simple version of breakfast grits with bacon and sliced tomatoes I'd eaten during a visit to Falls Mill, to a haute cheddar-bound version laden with peppery chorizo oil and slivers of mushroom that I'd found at a Nashville hotel, and every plate in between, including the ones eaten at Crook's Corner (by far the most memorable), I was determined to master my own version of the classic.

My first attempt at making them myself left me overwhelmed with options. The occasion was that my close friend Jenn was visiting from Boston, and I decided we'd celebrate by making the dish with grits from one of the growing selection of bags within my freezer.

Before she arrived, I pored over recipes and ran through my notes to see which version would be both easy to execute (there would be children underfoot) and also fun for us to prepare together. There were the recipes I'd come to know by heart: Bill

Neal's shrimp and grits, the one featured in *The New York Times*, called for mushrooms, bacon, scallions, and Tabasco over a base of cheese grits; or there was Hoppin' John's version, which called for green bell peppers and onions. I looked to *The Lee Bros. Charleston Kitchen* by Matt and Ted Lee, and found that they use tomatoes, calling it a traditional Charleston addition.

In the book *Glorious Grits*, author Susan McEwen McIntosh (the sister of Frank McEwen, owner of McEwen & Sons, who supplies the grits used regularly by Frank Stitt at Highlands Bar & Kitchen in Birmingham) included eight different recipes for shrimp and grits, ranging from the basic breakfast shrimp and grits (bacon crumbled over top and heavy cream to finish the grits) to an "anniversary" version made with Gruyère in the grits and andouille sausage and white wine cooked in with the shrimp. And, of course, I checked every option offered forth in Nathalie Dupree's comprehensive *Shrimp & Grits Cookbook*.

There seemed to be as many recipes as there were food writers on my shelf, leaving me a little out of sorts as I tried to suss out which would act as my road map. But ultimately, what I wanted was to stand in the kitchen alongside my good friend, drink a nice glass of wine, and work our way through the steps of chopping, slicing, sautéing, and stirring, with the end result being a good memory and a collaborative creation. I wasn't necessarily looking for "authentic" or even fancy. I just wanted something that we could make and enjoy together—a one-time experience that neither of us could replicate, that spoke to the moment we were in, which was precious, because our visits and time together were becoming fewer and farther between.

So I decided I would improvise. I'd pull in a little bit of several recipes and create something that was entirely our own. Jenn's visit was timed for early summer, so I was able to track down fresh wild-caught Gulf shrimp. For the grits, I chose a bag of Falls Mills coarse white grits. I knew we wouldn't have to add much, but I did want to include a little cheese and cream to give the grits some depth of flavor. I picked up a little andouille, some mushrooms, an onion, and an extra bottle of white wine and got ready for our night of cooking.

I'd planned our meal for the last night of Jenn's visit. At the time, we were still living in our tiny, two-bedroom bungalow and Jenn had already endured three nights on our lumpy pull-out couch, which sat outside the kids' bedroom, where I'm certain she would have preferred more privacy. But we were both sad to see her trip coming to a close, and looked forward to one last lingering conversation over the stove.

To start, I'd already soaked the grits in a few cups of water and told Jenn to start cooking those while I deveined the shrimp. The shrimp were big, slippery, and so fresh that I had to cut deep into the flesh to pull out the veins, leaving open-flapped wings on their backs. The two pounds I'd purchased ended up yielding us about two dozen bite-size beauties—but it took me almost thirty minutes to get through the pile. I set them aside and looked over to Jenn, who had carefully drained the grits, measured out eight fresh cups of water, and was standing over the pot waiting for the water to come to a simmer.

"They like to be stirred—a lot," I said, handing her a spoon.

"I've never made grits!" she announced, amused at her own discovery. A born-and-bred Massachusetts girl, she'd grown up on pancakes with true maple syrup, not piles of buttered grits. She was intrigued with the pot that was starting to burble before her. I stepped away as she started stirring.

A few minutes later, after slicing the sausage and mushrooms and setting my pan over a flame, I looked down into the pot of grits and realized that Jenn had the heat set on high. I snapped up the wooden spoon she'd left on the counter and felt my way toward the bottom, realizing what I'd feared: the grits were sticking to the pot, developing a thick, overcooked crust on the bottom. Jenn looked over my shoulder, horrified.

"I can fix this," she said anxiously as she dug around in my drawer for a rubber spatula. "I just need to stir." She lowered the heat on the burner and dunked her spatula into the mix. I watched as she put her face in close to the pot and inhaled. "I've got this," she reassured me, shooing me to back off a bit.

I turned my attention back to cooking the shrimp and sausage mixture. Once the onions hit the pan, the smell wafted up, causing both Jenn and me to reach for our glasses of wine. We chatted as we cooked, about my kids, about her dog, about her husband, Max. The conversation veered from topic to topic, calling out people and memories from our past. All the while, Jenn stirred, leaning up against the counter to take a load off her feet. She'd been at it for nearly an hour now, and noticed me constantly checking on her progress. At one point, she pulled the spatula up.

"No more sticking," she said proudly. We each dipped a spoon into the pot and tasted, letting the steaming grits spread across our tongues.

"Needs salt," she said.

"And cheese," I replied.

We started to add things to the grits a little at a time. A few

pinches of salt and grinds from the pepper mill. I added a handful of shredded cheddar cheese and a splash of whipping cream.
Jenn stirred these together until the swirls of cheese and cream
blended into a creamy mirage inside the pot.

After a splash of white wine and a sprinkle of thyme leaves,
the shrimp were ready. The fragrant, bubbling mixture let out
wave after wave of salty, scented air.

Jenn's pot of grits, meanwhile, was starting to look like a luscious pool of golden goodness. She kept dipping her spoon in for
small tastes, and I could see that she'd added more salt and
pepper, as well as a few good pats of butter. I leaned over and
swiped my finger into the pot, licking it clean with my eyes
closed. I smiled.

"You make good grits," I said, causing her to laugh.

"I'm just good at following directions," she said, smiling.

Dave, our kids, Charlie and Maggie, and our dog, Rex, had
been slowly circling around the small kitchen for the past hour,
trying to get under and around us, peering into pots and pans
whenever we would give them a chance. Just as the ravenous whine
of starving children reached a dull roar, we pulled out the dinner
plates. Jenn started by ladling a large pile of grits onto each plate,
then handed each to me to top with a few spoonfuls of the shrimp
and gravy. I sprinkled a few coarsely chopped fresh parsley leaves
on top to add color.

Jenn and I sat down, at last, and poured ourselves more wine.
With a toast, we celebrated our cooking skills, our friendship, and
grits . . . then pulled our forks through our creation to take a bite.
I smiled, mouth shut, enjoying the pure pleasure of the flavors
that sank into my tongue. I reveled in the comfort, not just of the

food and warmth of the dish, but in having my close friend beside me. The look on her face mirrored mine and we smiled at each other once again, grateful that this comforting plate of food was an opportunity to come together.

As we ate and drank and laughed, I started to tell Jenn how I was feeling about the South and how my life had changed since moving there. My research was still in progress, but I knew by that point that having a better understanding of grits had given me the tools to help shape a more complete picture of the South for myself. It was no longer the images of red ants or me needing a translator at the grocery store. Instead, I saw the South as a series of never-ending stories, told from millions of different perspectives—all of them true and revelatory.

What I'd come to understand was that the South, in all its iterations and corners, hollers and plateaus, was a deeply layered and complex place, but one that was also lovely and inspiring. There were people across the South, I'd learned, who were intentionally and diligently working to preserve the past, and carry on certain traditions and rituals—all with a respect for history, as well as a desire to do better going forward. Many of the people I'd met were consciously aware of the past, and were determined not only to avoid making the same mistakes that had been made before, but also, in their own way, to try to make amends for those wrongs that had already occurred.

From Glenn Roberts, Sean Sherman, and Greg Johnsman to Julia Tatum, Lawrence Burwell, and Philip Ranck, every story had given me a new perspective, introduced me to a corner of new knowledge, and helped shape a bigger story about this region. Some of those stories made me uncomfortable with my own place in this world, and my own whiteness. Other stories gave me end-less hope for the direction in which this version of the South was headed. And others just made me hungry, made me crave a seat at the table, wanting to find my own place in this ongoing story of the South.

My meal with Jenn that night left me both satisfied and sati-ated. The cooking, the wine, the conversation, the laughter—we savored it all, but none so much as the pile of grits we'd prepared together. They were special because they were something shared. And eating them, I understood that it was the sharing of grits—and, thereby, the sharing of stories—that was going to continue to help me understand the South, and all the nuances contained within it that I still had left to discover.

SHRIMP AND GRITS FOR COMPANY

Serves 6 to 8

Grits

2 cups grits

8 cups water

Pinch of salt

1 cup grated cheddar cheese

Heavy cream

Shrimp

1 pound smoked andouille sausage, sliced

1 onion, minced

8 ounces mushrooms, sliced

Salt

1 pound wild-caught shrimp, peeled and deveined

¾ cup dry white wine

2 tablespoons butter

1 tablespoon chopped fresh thyme leaves

Squeeze of lemon juice

Freshly ground black pepper

MAKE THE GRITS: Place the grits in a bowl and fill with water. Let sit for about 1 hour. Drain the grits and place them in a large pot. Add the 8 cups water and set over medium heat. Stir as mixture comes to a simmer. Reduce the heat to low, add the salt, and cook until the grits are tender, 40 to 45 minutes. Add the cheese and cream and stir to combine. Keep warm, adding more water or cream to keep grits loose until ready to serve.

MAKE THE SHRIMP: In a large skillet, cook the sausage over medium-high heat until browned, 5 to 7 minutes. Remove from the pan and set aside.

Add the onion and mushrooms to the skillet with a pinch of salt. Cook over medium-high heat, stirring, until softened, about 5 minutes. Add the shrimp and cook until they are pink, about 3 minutes. Add the wine, butter, and thyme and simmer until the wine has reduced by half, about 2 minutes. Remove from the heat and season with lemon juice, salt, and pepper.

To serve, spoon the grits into a shallow serving bowl. Top with the shrimp mixture and sausage slices, and serve.

⟨⟩❊⟨⟩

BAKED GRITS JAMBALAYA

Serves 6 to 8

Inspired by a recipe in the book Glorious Grits *by author Susan Mc-Ewen McIntosh, I make this jambalaya with grits instead of rice, and bake it, both for ease of cooking and to give the grits a bit of a crackly crunch.*

3 tablespoons vegetable oil

1 pound boneless chicken thighs

1 pound smoked andouille sausage, cut into 1-inch-thick slices

1 onion, chopped

1 green bell pepper, chopped

2 celery stalks, chopped

8 ounces mushrooms, coarsely chopped (about 2 cups)

1½ teaspoons salt

½ teaspoon freshly ground black pepper

2 garlic cloves, minced

½ teaspoon red pepper flakes

2 cups stone-ground grits

3 cups beef broth

1 (14.5-ounce) can diced tomatoes

2 tablespoons butter

1 (8-ounce) can tomato sauce

½ cup water

4 scallions, chopped

2 tablespoons chopped fresh parsley leaves

1 tablespoon Creole seasoning

Fresh thyme leaves

Preheat the oven to 350ºF.

In a Dutch oven with a lid, heat the oil over medium-high heat. Brown chicken thighs, about 3 minutes per side. Remove from the pan and coarsely chop. Set aside.

Add the sausage to Dutch oven and cook until just starting to brown, 5 to 7 minutes. Remove from the pan and set aside. Add the onion, bell pepper, celery, mushrooms, 1 teaspoon of the salt, and ½ teaspoon of the black pepper and cook until vegetables are softened, 5 to 7 minutes. Stir in the garlic and red pepper flakes and cook until fragrant, about 30 seconds.

Return the chicken and sausage to pan. Add the grits, broth, diced tomatoes, and butter and stir to combine. Bring to a simmer, stirring, until the butter has melted. Cover the Dutch oven and transfer to the oven. Bake for 30 minutes, stirring once about halfway through and scraping the brown bits from the bottom of the pan.

Meanwhile, in a medium bowl, combine the tomato sauce, water, half the scallions, the parsley, and the Creole seasoning. After 30 minutes, uncover the Dutch oven and add the tomato sauce mixture, stirring thoroughly and once again scraping up the browned bits. Bake for 15 minutes more, or until the grits are cooked through and tender. Fluff with a spoon or fork. Garnish with the remaining scallions and serve.

ACKNOWLEDGMENTS

I am so very grateful for the work of my editor, Daniela Rapp, for both planting the seed for this book and then helping me bring it all together. My agent, Danielle Chiotti, a friend, collaborator, and confidante, also played a vital role in bringing this book to life.

I'm thankful to have friends within the Southern Foodways Alliance who helped usher early versions of this work, including John T. Edge and Osayi Endolyn. They also gave me an introduction to the magic of Rivendell Writers' Colony, which is currently without a home but lives on in spirit—much of this book came to fruition there. Carmen Toussaint, your presence was essential.

I owe a great deal of thanks to several early guides who gifted me with suggestions, glimpses of their own research, contacts, and in some cases, warm beds, including Alice Randall, Nancie

McDermott, Ronni Lundy, Sheri Castle, Thomas Williams, and Elizabeth Sims. I owe a lot to those who have researched and written about grits before me. There are too many to mention, but Bill Neal, Bill Perry, and Betty Fussell wrote essential texts, and their words were ones I turned to often in my research.

I'm also thankful for the patient readers and researchers who lent their eyes and expertise, including Kim Green, Sheila Martin, and Virginia Anderson. My research was facilitated by so many, including the millers, chefs, and growers who gave interviews, as well as archive specialist Ceri McCarron at the Jimmy Carter Presidential Library, Nicole LaFlamme and Brian Huston from the J. M. Smucker Company, the good librarians at the Nashville Public Library, and the creators of Newspapers.com.

While writing this book, I often found myself on the road but with access to serene writing spaces—including several branches of the Nashville Public Library, coffee shops all over the South, and the homes of friends and family who took me in, including Joe and Cathy Fanelli; my sister Shannon; my parents, Dottie and Kelly; my in-laws, Becky and Dave Murray; and close friends Carol and Jim Williams. Thanks to all of you for offering me not only moral support but also a comfortable seat, a bed, a meal, a drink, a babysitter, and sometimes even the gift of a silent space.

I could not have survived the emotional roller coaster of the writing process without my collaborators, dirty page collectors, road warriors, and dear friends Jennifer Justus and Cindy Wall. From afar, my support squad, including Jenn Sederer, Karen Lennon, Nicole Kanner, and all the Syracuse girls, and closer to home, Trisha Boyer, encouraged and gave me strength, as always.

And, of course, I am tremendously grateful for those who quietly put up with me while I went into writer mode. Dave, Charlie, and Maggie: You are my greatest motivation and inspiration. I couldn't do this work without your tolerance, your support, your unconditional love, your appreciation for grits, and your wealth of hugs—thank you for all of it, and for allowing and encouraging me to do what I love.

FURTHER READING

My research for this book was extensive and far-reaching, but these are the texts, books, interviews, films, and articles that stood out for giving me a deeper understanding of grits and of the South.

Barber, Dan. *The Third Plate: Field Notes on the Future of Food*. Penguin, 2014.

Bennett, Richard. *History of Corn Milling*. Simpkin, Marshall, and Company, Ltd. 1898.

Best, Bill. *Saving Seeds, Preserving Taste: Heirloom Seed Savers in Appalachia*. Ohio University Press, 2013.

Bjerga, Alan, with Jeremy Diamond and Cindy Hoffman. "The Crop that Ate America," *Bloomberg*, May 11, 2017.

Bower, Anne L. (editor). *African American Foodways*. University of Illinois Press, 2007.

Brock, Sean. *Heritage*. Artisan, 2014.

Catledge, Turner. "The Meaning of True Grits," *The New York Times*, January 31, 1982.

Claiborne, Craig. "Barbecue: Southern State of the Art," *The New York Times*, April 25, 1984.

Claiborne, Craig. "Concoctions with Corn," *The New York Times*, April 18, 1965.

Claiborne, Craig. "Dining in a Southern Mansion: She-Crab Soup and Grits Souffle," *The New York Times*, March 2, 1967.

Claiborne, Craig. "For a Carolina Chef, Helpings of History," *The New York Times*, July 10, 1985.

Claiborne, Craig. "Grits: Moving North to Appear on Some Very Chic Menus," *The New York Times*, August 11, 1976.

Claiborne, Craig. "They've Gussied Up Those Hominy Grits," *The New York Times*, September 15, 1967.

Dabney, Joseph E. *Smokehouse Ham, Spoon Bread & Scuppernog Wine: The Folkore and Art of Southern Appalachian Cooking.* Cumberland House Publishing, 1998.

Douglass, Frederick. *Narrative of the Life of Frederick Douglass.* Anti-Slavery Office, 1845.

Dupree, Nathalie. *Nathalie Dupree's Shrimp and Grits Cookbook.* Gibbs Smith, 2006.

Dupree, Nathalie. *New Southern Cooking.* Knopf, 1986.

Dupree, Nathalie, with Cynthia Graubart. *Mastering the Art of Southern Cooking.* Gibbs Smith, 2012.

Dyer, Ceil. *The Carter Family Favorites Cookbook.* Delacorte Press, 1977.

Edgar, Walter. *Walter Edgar's Journal* podcast. SCETV, November 9, 2012.

Edge, John T. (editor). *The New Encyclopedia of Southern Culture, Vol. 7, Foodways.* University of North Carolina Press, 2007.

Edge, John T. *The Potlikker Papers: A Food History of the Modern South.* Penguin, 2017.

Egerton, John. *Southern Food: At Home, On the Road, In History.* Alfred A. Knopf, 1987.

Ferris, Marci Cohen. *The Edible South: The Power of Food and the Making of an American Region.* University of North Carolina Press, 2016.

Fussell, Betty. *Crazy for Corn.* HarperCollins, 1995.

Fussell, Betty. *The Story of Corn.* Alfred A. Knopf, 1992.

Haller, Henry, with Virginia Aronson. *The White House Family Cookbook: Two*

Decades of Recipes, a Dash of Reminiscence, and a Pinch of History from America's Most Famous Kitchen. Random House, 1987.

Harder, Jules Arthur. *The Physiology of Taste: Practical American Cookery in Six Volumes*. San Francisco, 1885.

Harris, Jessica B. *High on the Hog: A Culinary Journey from Africa to America*. Bloomsbury USA, 2012.

Hazard, Jessie. "Without intervention of some of Charleston's smartest culinary minds, an heirloom kernel would have vanished," *Charleston City Paper*, March 2, 2016.

Head, Thomas. "Southern Staple Steps Up to the Plate," *Nation Restaurants News*, September 29, 2008.

Lee, Matt and Ted Lee. *The Lee Bros. Charleston Kitchen*. Clarkson Potter, 2013.

Lee, Matt and Ted Lee. *The Lee Bros. Southern Cookbook*. Martens Maxwell, 2006.

Lewis, Edna, with Scott Peacock. *The Gift of Southern Cooking: Recipes and Revelations from Two Great American Cooks*. Alfred A. Knopf, 2003.

Lovett, John N. Jr. *Falls Mill: A Legacy of Power and Industry*. Self-published, 2010.

Lundy, Ronni. *Victuals: An Appalachian Journey, with Recipes*. Clarkson Potter, 2016.

Marsh, Carole. *Grits R Us Cookbook*. Gallopade International, 1987.

McGee, Marty. *Meadows Mills: The First Hundred Years*. Self-published, 2001.

McIntosh, Susan McEwan. *Glorious Grits*. Oxmoor House, 2009.

Melanson, Dave. "Power from a Partnership," *UKNow University News*, January 23, 2017.

Miller, Adrian E. *Soul Food: The Surprising Story of an American Cuisine, One Plate at a Time*. University of North Carolina Press, 2013.

Moss, Robert. "The Suprisingly Recent Story of How Shrimp and Grits Won Over the South," *Serious Eats*, August 14, 2014.

Neal, Bill. *Bill Neal's Southern Cooking*. University of North Carolina Press, 1985.

Neal, Bill, and Bill Perry. *Good Old Grits*. Workman, 1991.

Neal, Moreton. *Remembering Bill Neal*. University of North Carolina Press, 2004.

Opala, Joseph A. "The Gullah: Rice, Slavery, and the Sierra-Leone American Connection," *African American Foodways*, University of Illinois Press, 2007.

Pierce, Donna Battle. "Sweets versus Savory Grits? A Food Historian Settles Debate," *Ebony*, May 27, 2016.

Plemmons, Tony, and Nancy Plemmons. *Cherokee Cooking From the Mountains and Gardens to the Table*. Self-published, 2000.

Robinson, Sallie Ann. *Gullah Home Cooking the Daufuskie Way*. University of North Carolina Press, 2003.

Shields, David. *Southern Provisions: The Creation and Revival of a Cuisine*. University of Chicago Press, 2015.

Smart-Grosvenor, Vertamae. *Vibration Cooking or, The Travel Notes of a Geechee Girl*. University of Georgia Press, 2011.

Sohn, Mark F. *Appalachian Home Cooking: History, Culture and Recipes*. University of Kentucky Press, 2005.

Tartan, Beth, and Rudy Hayes. *Miss Lillian and Friends: The Plains, Georgia, Family Philosophy and Recipe Book*. A&W Publishing, 1977.

Willis, Virginia. *Grits*. Short Stack Editions, 2013.

Wilson, Gilber L. *Buffalo Bird Woman's Garden*. Minnesota Historical Society Press, 1987. (Originally published as *Agriculture of the Hidatsa Indians: An Indian Interpretation*. University of Minnesota, 1917.)

Woodward, Stan. *Hallowed Ground: Primitive Camp Meetings of the South Carolina Low Country*. Southern Culture and Folklife Documentaries, 2002.

Woodward, Stan. *It's Grits*. Southern Culture and Folklife Documentaries, 1980.

NOTES

1. Anson Mills website, ansonmills.com

2. Betty Fussell, *The Story of Corn* (Albuquerque: University of New Mexico Press, 1992).

3. Ibid., 197.

4. Adrian Miller, *Soul Food* (Chapel Hill: University of North Carolina Press, 2013).

5. Frederick Douglass, *Narrative of the Life of Frederick Douglass* (1845).

6. Interview with Michael Twitty, author, historian, and food writer.

7. Joseph A. Opala, *The Gullah: Rice, Slavery, and the Sierra Leone–American Connection* (United States Information Service, 1987).

8. Fussell, *The Story of Corn*, 213.

9. Dave Melanson, "Power from a Partnership," *UKNow*, http://uknow.uky.edu/research/power-partnership

10. Miller, *Soul Food*, 29.

11. Ibid., 190–91.

12. Chapel Hill: University of North Carolina Press, 2014.

13. Headnote for "Old-Fashioned Creamy Grits," 170.

14. Alan Bjerga, Jeremy Diamond, and Cindy Hoffman, "The Crop That Ate America," *Bloomberg*, May 11, 2017.

15. Moreton Neal, *Remembering Bill Neal* (Chapel Hill: University of North Carolina Press, 2004).

16. In two other mentions of this moment in the same book, the year is listed as 1983. When Claiborne visited is never made clear, but the article, "Barbecue: Southern State of the Art," was published in *The New York Times* on April 25, 1984.

17. Moreton Neal, *Remembering Bill Neal*.

18. John T. Edge, *The Potlikker Papers* (New York: Penguin, 2017) 172–73.

19. Ibid., 187–88.

INDEX